A SHORT HISTORY
OF THE
EARLY CHURCH

by
Harry R. Boer

WILLIAM B. EERDMANS PUBLISHING COMPANY
GRAND RAPIDS, MICHIGAN

Library of Congress Cataloging in Publication Data

Boer, Harry R.
  A short history of the early church.

  Bibliography: p. 178.
  Includes index.
  1. Church history—Primitive and early church, ca. 30-600.
I. Title.
BR165.B645 1975   270.1   75-25742
ISBN 0-8028-1339-9

A NOTE TO THE READER

We are pleased to make available this brief survey of early Christianity. Dr. Harry Boer has drawn upon his considerable experience as a missionary and teacher in Nigeria to prepare a concise and clearly written account of the people, places, institutions, events, and ideas that made a difference in the development of the Christian faith. Students who want a rapid review of this period of church history will find here a helpful resource. The questions for discussion at the end of each chapter enhance the book's potential as a study guide for church groups and individuals interested in learning more about early Christianity.

A large part of the story of these centuries deals with the bitter conflicts that arose over how precisely to confess what the church believed about the person of Jesus Christ. Although these doctrinal disputes were often hopelessly entangled with political power struggles, so that heresy and treason became indistinguishable, an understanding of the theology of the situation is crucial for an appreciation of what concerned the early Christians and why later church history took the course it did. And so, it is a primary concern of Dr. Boer to convey the theological essence of these disagreements.

Another important facet of the story of the early church has to do with its institutionalization and its rise to a position of significance in the Roman empire. Time and again these chapters tell of the continued hostility of the world to the church — whether that opposition took the form of persecuting the church and making martyrs of the saints or of accepting the church, establishing it, and trying to use it for self-serving ends foreign to the entire thrust of the gospel of Jesus Christ.

As it confronted the reality of living in that kind of world, the church developed regular leadership positions. The persons who filled these roles — many of them encountered in this book — were all very human, subject to motives of personal gain, but also capable by God's grace of heroism in the face of incredible opposition and of thought about the faith so profound that it still grips us today.

To read the story of these years, Dr. Boer suggests, is to feel grateful for the gifts God has given the church from the outset, but humbled by the record of what the church has often made of those gifts. Beyond this, however, is a renewed feeling of confidence in the guidance still offered the church by its Savior and Head. We trust this short account will not only enlighten the reader about the church but stimulate such a sense of appreciation for God's grace toward his people.

THE PUBLISHERS

CONTENTS

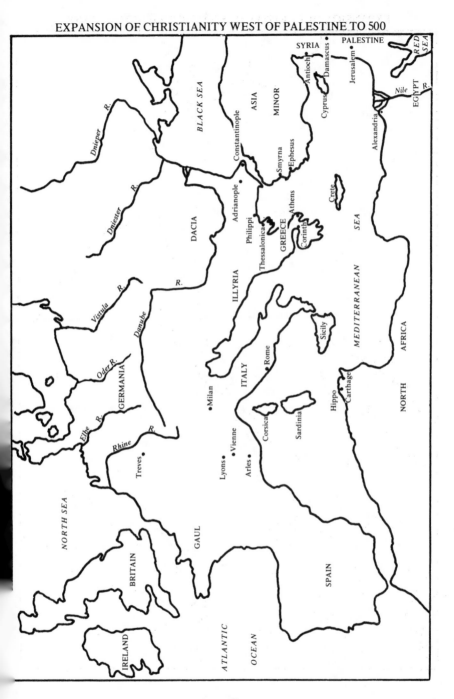

EXPANSION OF CHRISTIANITY WEST OF PALESTINE TO 500

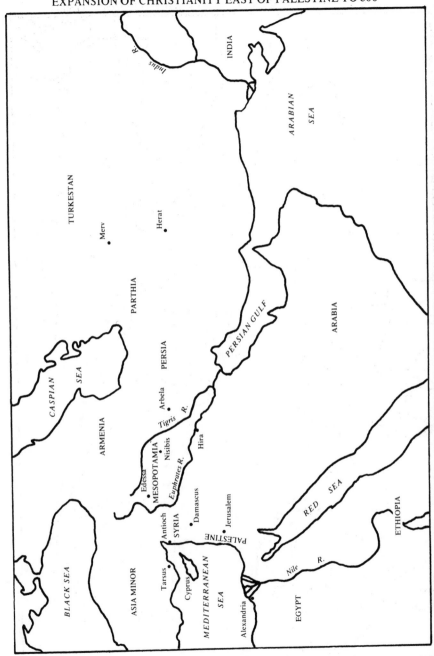

FIFTH CENTURY MIGRATIONS INTO THE EMPIRE

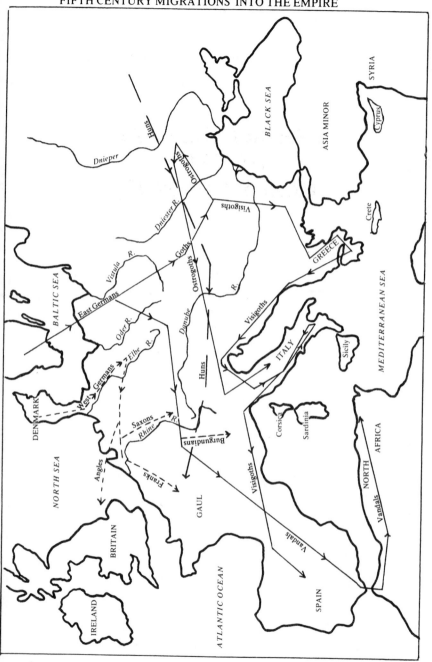

A SHORT HISTORY
OF THE
EARLY CHURCH

CHAPTER I

THE WORLD OF THE EARLY CHURCH

The Christian church was born in a world that was already old. Great empires had risen and fallen. The glories of Egypt, Sumer, Babylon, Assyria, Persia, and Greece lay centuries in the past. Now it was Rome, the greatest of the ancient empires, that governed the civilized world. It was almost exclusively in that empire that the Christian church lived the first five centuries of its life. Before beginning a discussion of the history of the church, it is important to note briefly the main characteristics of the world in which it developed. In doing so, mention should be made of the Roman Empire, the Jewish background of the church, the influence of Greek thought, and the various kinds of religion that Christianity found in its environment.

THE ROMAN EMPIRE

The Christian church was born in the Roman Empire. This great and powerful commonwealth stretched from England to Persia and from the Sahara to northwestern Germany. The Mediterranean Sea was not then, as it is now, a sea touching the shores of many nations. It was rather a great inland waterway uniting the many provinces of the empire that surrounded it on all sides. Hundreds of tribes lived within Rome's borders, and nations with a history far longer than that of Rome were under its control. The center of the empire was the city of Rome, and in Rome all the power of government was in the hands of the emperor.

1. Growth

At the birth of Jesus, Rome was about seven hundred and fifty years old. It had been founded as a small village on the banks of the Tiber River in western Italy. It grew to become a town, a city, and a small state. By means of wars and treaties with neighboring states, it continued to expand.

In 265 B.C., five hundred years after its founding, Rome was master of the Italian peninsula. It then reached out westward across the sea. In less than a hundred years it had conquered the islands of Sicily, Corsica, Sardinia, the powerful state of Carthage in North Africa, and much of Spain. Thereupon it turned eastward and northward. It conquered all the remaining lands around the Mediterranean Sea, all of Gaul to the north, and parts of modern Germany. In the course of this expansion, Palestine came under the control of the empire in 63 B.C. and became a province in the empire in A.D. 6.

2. Government

Until 27 B.C. all Rome's territories were administered by a form of government known as a republic. In it the Roman senate was very powerful, and no single individual controlled the government. In 27 B.C., however, after disastrous civil wars lasting more than a hundred years, the full power of Rome was given into the hands of Gaius Octavianus, the nephew of Julius Caesar (conqueror of Gaul and one of the greatest Romans). Octavianus is known in history as Caesar Augustus, first and greatest of the emperors. With him the republic ended and the empire began: he reigned from 27 B.C. to A.D. 14. He is the Caesar of whom it is written in Luke 2:1: "In those days a decree went out from Caesar Augustus that all the world should be enrolled." Except for some fighting at the frontiers of the empire, the reign of peace begun by Augustus lasted more than two hundred years. It was during these two centuries that the church, arising out of the life and work of our Lord, became an empire-wide witness to the gospel.

3. Boundaries

The boundaries of the empire were clear. On the west, its boundary was the Atlantic Ocean. From the Alps to the North Sea, the Rhine River separated Gaul from unconquered Germany; rising in southwestern Germany, not far from the source of the Rhine, the Danube River flowed eastward to the Black Sea. It protected the empire from the barbarian tribes to the north. In the east the boundary was the Persian Empire. In the south, below the long, fertile strip along the North African coast, the Sahara desert bounded the empire. Except for a few variations, especially in the east (because of wars with Persia), these boundaries were maintained for more than four centuries.

4. Pax Romana
In this vast empire the *pax Romana* (Roman peace) made trade and travel both easy and safe. By land, sea, and river it was possible to travel from one end of the empire to the other. It also encouraged the development of culture in every way, leading to great achievements in literature, architecture, and sculpture. The study of law was greatly developed. The economy provided varying degrees of prosperity throughout the empire. Everywhere the Roman army was a symbol of Roman power, Roman law, and Roman peace. Not least, there was a common language — Greek — in which one could communicate in the larger part of the empire. A careful reading of the book of Acts will reveal many of the characteristics of the Roman Empire mentioned in this section.*

THE JEWISH BACKGROUND

The roots of the Christian church reach back deeply into the history and religion of Israel. "Salvation," said Jesus, "is from the Jews" (John 4:22). Jesus came not to destroy but to fulfil the law and the prophets (Matt. 5:17). Those who belong to Christ are Abraham's offspring, heirs according to the promise (Gal. 3:29). As Palestine was part of the Roman Empire, so the church is related, and very deeply so, to Israel, the people of Palestine. The earliest church was wholly Jewish, her Savior was a Jew, and the entire New Testament was probably written by Jews. It will therefore be useful to take brief note of Israel's history.

1. David to Alexander
The kingdom of Israel was founded by David, the son of Jesse, in about 1000 B.C. He reigned until about 960 B.C. David placed such a stamp on the kingdom and upon the kingly office that he became a symbol of Israel's later messianic hopes. After the death of his son Solomon in about 930 B.C., the kingdom David had established was split into two parts.

*Cf. chapters 10:1-2; 21:27-40; 23:16-35; 26:30-32; 27:1-8; 28:11-16.

The northern part, called Israel, was taken into Assyrian exile
in 721 B.C. It was never restored. The southern kingdom,
Judah, which had remained true to the house of David, had
a longer history. In 586 B.C., however, it too went into exile
in Babylon. In 539, Cyrus, king of Persia, conquered Babylon.
He allowed any exile who wished to return to Jerusalem to do
so. The following year a number of them returned to their
native land. These returnees in time rebuilt the temple,
which Nebuchadnezzar, king of Babylon, had destroyed.

After the first return, other groups went back to Palestine.
One of their leaders was Ezra, a priest who was deeply devoted to the Mosaic law. It was his strong desire to make
the observance of the Torah, Israel's law, a living part of
Jewish religion again. The Pharisees, whom we meet so often
in the Gospels and the book of Acts, grew out of the movement to restore the law that Ezra had begun.

Between 334 and 323 B.C., Alexander, the young
Macedonian king, conquered all lands east of Greece up to
India and as far south as Egypt. When he died in 323 B.C.,
his generals divided among themselves the empire he had
created. Ptolemy became ruler of Egypt. His area of authority
included Palestine, and it remained under the authority of his
house until 198 B.C. In that year, the house that had descended
from another general, Seleucis, gained control of Palestine.
The Seleucids governed Syria, much of Asia Minor, and all of
Persia. This change in the government of Palestine had very
great consequences for the Jewish people.

2. The Maccabees

The Ptolemaic kings had permitted the Jews to practice
their religion freely. For more than two hundred and fifty
years after their return from exile, the Jews had observed
the Mosaic law as Ezra had taught it to them. Now their
new masters pressed them to surrender their ancient religion
and follow Greek ways. The leader of this movement was
Antiochus the Fourth, the Seleucid king of Syria. He came to
the throne in 175 B.C. When the Jews resisted his policies,
riots and massacres resulted. The Jewish religion was forbidden, Greek religion was enforced, prostitutes were brought
into the temple, and Jewish ceremony was prohibited, especially circumcision. Most offensive of all, the Torah
was openly burnt.

The rebellion against Seleucid rule that now broke out in full strength (163 B.C.) was led by an aged priest named Mattathias and his four sons. Of these, Judas was the leader. Together they are known as the Maccabees, that is, men who fight violently. In 141 the Jews gained complete victory over their Seleucid enemies, and for the first time since 586 B.C. Israel again became an independent nation. She kept her freedom only eighty years. In 63 B.C., civil war in Palestine gave occasion to Rome to establish her authority there. For the next sixty years Israel was semi-independent, her rulers being appointed by Rome. In 37 B.C., Herod (known as Herod the Great, during whose reign Jesus was born) became king with Rome's approval. After his death, the kingdom was divided among his sons. Archelaus received Judea, Samaria, and Idumea; Herod Antipas received Galilee and Perea; and Philip received the area northeast of Galilee. In A.D. 6, Archelaus was deposed because of misconduct and sent into exile. His area became a Roman province and was governed by Roman procurators. From A.D. 26-36, the procurator of Judea was a Roman named Pontius Pilate.

In conclusion, a word must be said about the rise of the synagogue, the Sanhedrin, the Pharisees and Sadducees, and about the Jewish dispersion in the ancient world.

3. Synagogue and Sanhedrin

Before the Jewish exile in 586 B.C., the center of Jewish worship was the temple in Jerusalem. After the exile, the center of Jewish worship was the synagogue found in every local community of Jews. It had existed in Palestine before the exile. In Babylonia the Jews, deprived of the temple, emphasized the synagogue for purposes of prayer, the reading of the scriptures, and teaching, more than they had done in the homeland. It was further developed and strengthened by Ezra and his successors as a means of teaching the law. The book of Acts indicates that where there were Jews in the empire there was a synagogue also. It was from the synagogue that Paul began his witness in any city he visited. The leader or president of the assembly was called the ruler of the synagogue. He was assisted by a reader of the scriptures, a leader in congregational prayer, and an officer who had custody of the scriptures and presided in the absence of the ruler.

The governing body of the Jews in Palestine was the San-

hedrin. Literally, the word "Sanhedrin" means to "sit together." Although it was under Roman authority, it governed
the province in both civil and religious matters. In matters
that were solely religious, the Jews outside Palestine recognized its authority. The Sanhedrin was composed largely of
Sadducees and Pharisees under the leadership of the high
priest.

4. Pharisees and Sadducees

The Pharisees and the Sadducees were the Jewish leaders
from the time of the Maccabees onward. The Sadducees came
from priestly families and were lawyers; they favored old ways
and were opposed to change. Nevertheless, they supported
efforts of the later Maccabees to introduce Greek ideas into
Jewish life. In religion, they are chiefly known as denying
the doctrine of the resurrection and the existence of angels
and spirits. They also believed that the soul perished with
the body. Thus there was for them no future life.

In nearly all respects the Pharisees opposed the Sadducees. They were not a priestly class but were laymen. They
too were lawyers, but they believed that the law should be
open to new interpretations. The Pharisees were ardent nation-
alists and therefore opposed foreign influences, whether Greek
or Roman. They believed in the resurrection and in a future
life with rewards and punishments. They were chiefly concerned with the outward observance of the law, in which
spiritual attitudes played little part. It was especially this aspect of their religion that brought them into conflict with Jesus.
The Sadducees had wrong doctrines; the Pharisees had right
doctrines, but their lives contradicted their teachings. Therefore, Jesus could say, "The scribes and the Pharisees sit on
Moses' seat; so practice and observe whatever they tell you,
but not what they do; for they preach, but do not practice"
(Matt. 23:2, 3).

The Sadducees lost influence and gradually disappeared
after the fall of Jerusalem in A.D. 70. The Pharisees carried
on for a time, but they too disappeared from the scene with the
destruction of the Jewish state.

5. The Dispersion

So far, our consideration of Judaism has been limited to

Palestine. It is important to note, however, that there were many more Jews outside Palestine than there were in it. Deportations of prisoners of war, but especially the interest of commerce, spread Jews in all directions from Palestine. It is estimated that during the time of the early Roman Empire there were about two and one-half million Jews in Palestine. There were one million in each of the areas of Egypt, Asia Minor, and Mesopotamia, in addition to about one hundred thousand in Italy and North Africa. Smaller colonies were scattered throughout the empire. The New Testament reference to the Dispersion is impressive: John 7:35, Acts 2:5-11, with many other references throughout the book of Acts, James 1:1, I Peter 1:1. Inseparable from the Dispersion was the synagogue. Together they established a natural base outside Palestine for the missionary proclamation of the gospel.

The most important center of the Dispersion was Alexandria, Egypt. There the Jews occupied whole quarters of the city. There the Old Testament was translated into the Greek language in 250 B.C., thus making it available to the Greek-speaking world. It became known as the Septuagint. There also Jewish intellectual life found its greatest spokesman in the famous Jewish philosopher Philo — about 20 B.C. to A.D. 42 — to whom we shall return in the next section.

GREEK THOUGHT

Within the empire the most important spiritual influence came not from the Romans but from the Greeks. Roman power and Roman law controlled the military, political, social, and economic life of the empire; Greek thinking controlled the minds of men.

1. Early Greek Philosophers

Beginning in about 600 B.C., Greek philosophers thought profoundly about the nature of the world and the meaning of life. Thales was the first of the philosophers. He lived in the city of Miletus on the southwest coast of Asia Minor. He believed that all that existed arose in one way or another from water. Anaximander, a disciple of Thales, taught that not water but the boundless atmosphere was the source of everything. The philosophy of Heraclitus, who lived in about 500 B.C. in

Ephesus (also in Asia Minor), was more complex. The basic element of the universe, he said, is fire. Out of it all things arise, and to it all things return. Out of fire comes air; out of air, water; out of water, earth. Then earth returns to water, water to air, air to fire, and thus the endless cycle of change goes on and on. The combinations made possible by these changes cause the great variety of things that are found in the world. But none of them abides. There is nothing constant in life, nothing that is permanent. Life is like a flowing river: one can never step into the same water twice. Indeed, Heraclitus made the river a picture of his philosophy, which he summed up in the words "all things flow." Nevertheless, the constantly changing world is controlled by a mind, a reason which he called the *logos*. This word should be carefully noted, for it played a very large role in the theological thinking of the early church.

Thales, Anaximander, and Heraclitus all lived in Asia Minor, which had been colonized by Greeks. A similar Greek colony in southern Italy also produced philosophers. One of its leading figures was Parmenides. Living at the same time as Heraclitus, he taught the very opposite of the Ephesian philosopher: he believed that there is no change at all. There is only one thing that exists — being itself. All the change that we experience and observe is appearance only. The variety, the beauty, the sadness, and the joy of life are appearances that exist solely in our minds.

Strange as these views may seem, they presented a fundamental problem with which all serious thought about life must struggle. They raised the question: how are permanence and change, reality and appearance, eternity and time related to each other? How is the mature man related to the child out of which he grew? Change has made the child become a man, but permanence has kept the person the same. How is this to be understood?

2. Socrates and Plato

With Socrates, who lived in Athens about 450 B.C., a change took place in Greek thinking. He was more interested in the quality of men than in the nature of the world. Socrates taught that we can know only one thing with certainty: man himself. We can know what we ought to be and what the purpose of life is. To know this is to have true knowledge. This knowledge can be gained by proper education; man has the power to make himself morally good.

There now appeared in Greece two of the most distinguished philosophers of all time. They were Plato (about 425-345 B.C.), a disciple of Socrates, and Aristotle (about 385-320 B.C.), a disciple of Plato. The center of philosophical thinking had by this time shifted from the colonies to the motherland, specifically to Athens. When Rome was not yet fully master of Italy, when Palestine was still under Persian control, Athens was the brilliant cultural center of the world.

Plato united in one philosophy the concern of the earlier thinkers to understand the world as a whole and the concern of Socrates to understand man. With Parmenides, he believed that the real world was not the world that could be seen and felt — mountains, trees, sky, rivers, fields, men. The real world was the unseen world, the world of the ideas. By "ideas" Plato did not mean thoughts or opinions or what we refer to as "ideas." He meant spiritual realities that exist in an unseen world. In that world are the "ideas" of material things like tree, mountain, water, chair, and of spiritual qualities like courage, love, truth, goodness, and, not least, of the soul. These ideas exist in the unseen world in the order of their service to one another. At the very top of the pyramid is the Idea of the Good.

But there is also another world, the world of matter. In its original state matter is without form or shape. It is a disordered, unharmonious, formless mass, a chaos. However, we never see matter in that shapeless, formless way. The ideas stamp it with their character of order and meaning. It is this union of the perfect ideas with disordered matter that we see and experience in the world around us. Matter is the source of all evil—of pain, disappointment, imperfection, sorrow, and death. The whole world of nature and man comes out of the strange union of ideas and matter. This is the world of change that had impressed Heraclitus so deeply. All that is in the world is a poor copy of the eternal, true, unchanging ideas coming to expression through their union with matter. Whatever is beautiful, moral, fitting, and purposeful in these copies comes from the ideas. Whatever is evil, painful, and destructive in these copies is derived from matter. Both worlds are equally eternal; neither can ever gain a victory over the other.

Man is a union of spirit and matter. When death comes, the soul welcomes it, for it can then return to its pure state as idea unburdened by matter. It was for this reason that the philosophers in Athens listened quietly to Paul when he preached the gospel to them *until* he spoke about the resurrection: "Now when they heard of the resurrection of the dead, some mocked; but others said, 'We will hear you again about this' " (Acts 17:32).

In studying the history of the early church, it is necessary to understand this Greek view of the relationship between idea and matter, good and evil, soul and body. If it is not grasped, it is quite impossible to understand properly the first four centuries of church history. The two major heresies of Gnosticism and Arianism profoundly threatened the truth of the gospel, the first one before, the second one after A.D. 300. Both arose out of a misunderstanding of man and of the world after the fashion of Socrates and Plato. Only a scriptural view of God, of man, of the world, and of their relationships to each other saved the church from becoming a witness to a false gospel.

3. Stoicism

We must pass over the teachings of Aristotle and others to note briefly the major teachings of Stoicism. It was the dominant philosophy in the Roman Empire at the time of Christ and the early church.

The name Stoicism is derived from the Greek word *stoa,* meaning porch. It was a name applied to a public corridor near the market place in Athens where men could meet to discuss affairs. It was here that Zeno, a native of Cyprus, taught philosophy in about 300 B.C. His philosophy was named Stoicism after the place where he taught it. His teaching and that of his successors was, like Socrates', more concerned with human conduct than with the nature of the universe. He and his successors taught that only matter exists. There is no pure spirit: mind and body are both material. Even God is material; the universe is his body, and he is its soul. Stoicism, therefore, is a sort of pantheism, the teaching that all is God. Man is related to him as a drop of water is related to the ocean, as a spark is related to the fire out of which it shoots. God as the world-soul governs all things, loves men, and desires what is good for them.

Since man is related to God, he should follow where the divine reason, called the *logos,* leads. True wisdom and virtue consist in discovering where God's path for men lies. The truly human person does not resist God's leading; he surrenders himself to it however painful this may be, for God loves him. Virtue is one and is undivided. The four greatest qualities of character are wisdom, courage, moderation, and justice. If one lacks just one of these qualities, he lacks them all; if he truly has one, he truly has all. To be free and happy means to know oneself, to know God's will for oneself, and to live according to that knowledge.

Stoicism was religion as well as philosophy. But because it was philosophical in character, it was accepted only by educated men. The masses of the people were unable to reason things out as Stoicism required. Among the educated elements, however, some of the finest minds in the empire followed its teaching. One of these was Marcus Aurelius, emperor from A.D. 160-180. There was much in Stoicism that Christianity could and did use. But it could speak only to the educated. Even these, however, lacked the power to do what love and justice required. One of the cruelest persecutions of the empire against the church took place during the reign of Marcus Aurelius. The world therefore continued to wait for a religion that not only taught what was right but also provided the power to do what was right.

4. Philo

A philosopher whom we must note in conclusion is the Jewish thinker Philo. He was born about 20 B.C., died sometime after A.D. 40, and spent his life in Alexandria, the center of the Jewish Dispersion. In some respects Philo was more Greek than Jewish. He concerned himself with philosophy in a manner unusual for a Jew. He spoke and wrote Greek better than Hebrew. At the same time, he was and remained a genuine Jew. He found the highest divine authority not in philosophy but in the Old Testament, especially the Pentateuch. Indeed, Philo taught that whatever was true in the philosophy of the Greeks had been said earlier by the Jewish scriptures. He believed that somehow the Greeks had obtained their major ideas from the Old Testament.

Philo tried to combine the Old Testament scriptures with Greek philosophy in a united teaching. In doing this, he faced the problem of the doctrine of creation. According to biblical teaching God created the world out of matter. Greek philosophy could not allow this: God can have no contact with matter, the source of all evil. Therefore, Philo, like the Greeks, put a mediator between God and the world. This mediator he found in the *Logos*. He is the greatest of the powers with which God is surrounded. In him Philo saw a divine power that is less than God, standing between God and the world. Through him God has created all things. Later, this thought played a large role in the attempt of Christian thinkers to explain the relationship of Christ to God.

RELIGION IN THE EMPIRE

The various philosophical views undoubtedly satisfied many educated minds. The masses of the people, however, were not educated. How could they find fellowship and peace with God? These could be obtained only by religion. Even among the educated there was a feeling that philosophy could not provide final answers. There were many religions in the empire to meet these needs. They were broadly of three kinds.

1. Nature Religion

Nature religion saw supernatural power in mountains, lakes, rivers, trees, the sun and the moon, in certain animals and men. It honored forces in nature and believed in the power of amulets and charms. Beyond these there was belief in ancestors, in good and evil spirits, and in gods who controlled the destinies of men. Every religion of nature had its own myths and rituals and a special class of men named priests who could recite the myths and perform the ritual ceremonies. Nature religion was always group religion. The personal element was largely absent. In a simple agricultural, fishing, or herding society such a religion might seem to be adequate. For men living in a developing and swiftly changing world it was not. They needed religion in which the supernatural was more personal, a religion in which men could experience the supernatural in their troubled lives. This need was met by the mystery religions.

2. Mystery Religion

The great attractiveness of mystery religion lay in the

opportunity of fellowship with the divine that it offered. This fellowship was obtained by certain ceremonial acts. The first of these was *baptism,* whether with water or with the blood of an animal. This washed away uncleanness and made fellowship with the god possible. The baptism was followed by a *sacred meal,* in which this fellowship was experienced. The sacred meal led to *enlightenment.* In it the new believer received knowledge of the god into whose fellowship he had been baptized. In this enlightenment he also dedicated himself to the service of the god. Having this knowledge, the believer could live in peace and die in the comfort of reconciliation with his god. The followers of mystery religion were not allowed to reveal the secrets of baptism, meal fellowship, and enlightenment. For this reason the religion was called mystery religion.

Mystery religion had a long history in the East in India, Persia, Babylon, and Egypt. It was strong in the empire when Christianity began to spread. For a while one form of mystery religion, Mithraism, was a very strong competitor of Christianity and was especially favored by the Roman armies.

3. State Religion

State religion had strong political aspects. Its chief element was the making of sacrifice to the emperor. Originally, sacrifice had been made to the gods of the state. In the earlier years of the empire, sacrifices were made to dead emperors. Later, living emperors were worshiped with sacrifice. The emperor was regarded as the god who gave order and prosperity to the state; in him the empire was incarnated as it were. State religion was therefore regarded as uniting into one loyal community the great diversity of peoples and tribes in the empire. Any religion that recognized the god-emperor and did not interfere with good order in the empire was regarded as legitimate religion. State religion was, however, religion without warmth, without fellowship, without union with the divine and, especially, it was religion without salvation.

QUESTIONS FOR REVIEW

1. What are the three stages by which Rome developed from a village to an empire?

2. What is the significance of the Rhine and Danube rivers in the history of the Roman Empire? Through what countries do these rivers flow today?

3. Distinguish between the kingdoms of David, Israel, and Judah. What is the terminal date of each?

4. Who were the Seleucids, and what was the significance of their control of Palestine?

5. Compare the account of Jewish history from 37 B.C. (Herod) to A.D. 36 (Pilate) with Matthew 2; 3:1-3 and Luke 23:1-12.

6. What is meant by the Dispersion? Where was it strongest? How were synagogue and Sanhedrin related to it?

7. What important new element did Socrates introduce into Greek philosophic thinking?

8. What, according to Plato, was the relationship between the world of ideas and the world of matter?

9. In the teaching of Stoicism, why does the truly human person accept God's leading?

10. In what way was mystery religion in the empire superior to both nature and state religion?

CHAPTER II

THE BEGINNING OF THE CHURCH

It was in Palestine, the historic land of Israel, that the church of the New Testament first appeared in history. It is difficult to set a date for its beginning. If we say that the church began at Pentecost, we leave out of consideration the life and ministry of Jesus. If we say that the church began with him, we must remember the fact that the ministry of Jesus grew out of the life of Judaism. It is therefore best to say that the church arose out of the life and work of its Lord and became a universal witness to him at Pentecost.

THE MINISTRY OF JESUS

1. The Message

The message of Jesus was simple. He preached that the kingdom of God was at hand and that men could enter it through repentance and belief in the gospel (Mark 1:14, 15). The repentance Jesus required was for disobedience of the law of God. This law required men to love God above all and their neighbors as themselves (Matt. 22:34-40). Love is the fulfilling of the law. When disobedience causes a falling short of this love, repentance restores the balance between a man and his God and between a man and his neighbor. The Sermon on the Mount illustrates in many ways how man's vertical (man to God) and horizontal (man to man) relationships are to be maintained and strengthened. The gospel is the joyful news that God forgives those who repent, and he receives them as his children. At the same time, the preaching of Jesus was not an entirely new message. It arose out of and continued at a deeper level the message of the Old Testament (Matt. 5:17-20).

2. The Meaning

As Jesus performed his ministry he foresaw the unavoidable collision between his spiritual message and the message of external obedience taught by the Pharisees. He prepared for death and foretold it to his disciples (Mark 10:32-34). At the Passover feast, probably in the thirty-third year of his life, he suffered crucifixion. His death, however, was not simply a martyr's death. It was a saving death, full of life for those who see in it the full measure of obedience to the law of God. Through it he gave his life for the redemption of many. After his death he rose again in victory over death. Anyone who believes in him, though he die, yet shall he live, and whosoever lives and believes in him shall never die (John 11:25-26). Therefore, Paul preached with equal power "Jesus Christ and him crucified" (I Cor. 2:2), and "Jesus and the resurrection" (Acts 17:18).

3. The Mystery of Christ

From birth onward, the human and the divine were united in him. Yet their union was so natural that the one never seemed to be something additional or accidental to the other. He was born and grew up like other children. He increased in wisdom and in stature and in favor with God and man (Luke 2:52). He was hungry, tempted, tired, limited in knowledge; he could be indignant and angry, he was sociable and sympathetic, he prayed, and in the end he was crucified and killed.

At the same time, he repeatedly made claims and performed actions that were appropriate only to God. No one, he said, knows the Son except the Father, no one knows the Father except the Son, and anyone to whom the Son chooses to reveal him (Matt. 11:27). Before Abraham was, he is (John 8:58); he forgave sins, a prerogative of God alone (Mark 2:7); he received worship (John 20:28); he gave the Holy Spirit to his disciples (John 19:23); he is the Christ in whom messianic hopes are fulfilled (John 4:25, 26).

The church has seen profound mystery in these two aspects of the life of her Lord, but she has never seen anything strange or unnatural in them. She believes in Jesus, the incarnate Son of God, and preaches him to men. "Great indeed, we confess, is the mystery of our religion: He was manifested in the flesh, vindicated in the Spirit, seen by angels, preached among the nations, believed on in the world, taken up in glory" (I Tim. 3:16).

PENTECOST

The Old Testament had spoken again and again of the coming universal character of the people of God. The deepest ground for this expectation was the fact that the God who redeems is also the God who created all things. Although man has become sinful, the Creator does not abandon his work; he therefore restores it in redemption. The election of the people of Israel for special service had as its purpose the salvation of all the nations. Throughout the Old Testament, Israel's contact with the nations was maintained. Palestine itself was a crossroads between the great empires of her time. In his ministry Jesus predicted the spread of the gospel, but he did not, before his death, set forth a program of evangelism. This was given after his resurrection: "All authority in heaven and on earth has been given to me. Go therefore and make disciples of all nations, baptizing them in the name of the Father and of the Son and of the Holy Spirit, teaching them to observe all that I have commanded you; and lo, I am with you always, to the close of the age" (Matt. 28:18-20). This command, however, may not be separated from the coming of the Holy Spirit at Pentecost. The command to witness was not enough to create witnesses. There also had to be the conviction to witness and the power to witness. This was given to the church at Pentecost. At that time Christ returned to the church through the Holy Spirit to give it power and to be with it to the end of the age (Acts 1:6-8).

At Pentecost fundamental changes took place in the character and structure of the people of God:

a. The New Testament universal church replaced the strictly Israelite congregation as expressed in temple and synagogue.

b. The people of God ceased to be a national people and became an international, a universal community.

c. The preacher replaced the priest, the pulpit replaced the altar, and the church's witness to the sacrifice of Christ replaced the ceremonial sacrifice of animals.

The Jew's religious capital was Jerusalem, and he observed the law, the sabbath, and circumcision; the church has no capital city, no temple, no priest, no altar, no holy land. It is at home in every nation; where it is, its Lord is fully present, and it worships God in many forms.

This change in the outlook and structure of God's people did not become a full reality on the day of Pentecost. It took time for the church to understand that it was a universal fellowship. Even the apostle Peter came to understand it with difficulty. Some members of the church never understood it at all. Nevertheless, the speaking with tongues at Pentecost and the list of the nations reported in the second chapter of Acts indicate this basic change. Before another thirty years had passed, the gospel was established in Syria, Asia Minor, Greece, and Italy. It even had followers in Caesar's household in the capital of the empire.

PALESTINIAN CHRISTIANITY

We first meet the church as a body of believers in Jerusalem. At the Jewish feast of Pentecost, seven weeks after the crucifixion of Jesus, many were baptized as a result of the preaching of Peter. The church was thus from the beginning a sizable community. It lived its life in fellowship, worship, and mutual help, receiving new members daily (Acts 2:43-47). Its preaching was simple: repentance for sin, the death and resurrection of Christ, with strong emphasis on resurrection and baptism (Acts 2:29-42). This proclamation was accompanied by signs and wonders and the power of the Holy Spirit, resulting in many conversions, even among the priests.

1. Hellenist and Hebrew Christians

Soon after this promising beginning, Acts records two events that marred the fellowship of the church. The first was the sin of Ananias and Sapphira (Acts 5:1-11), the second the unhappiness of the Hellenists with their Hebrew brothers (Acts 6:1-6). The deceit of Ananias and Sapphira was tragic, but it did not arise out of the Christian community as a whole. The complaint of Hellenists against the Hebrews was quite a different matter. It indicated a significant difference within the church itself. It concerned a dispute between Christian Jews of Palestine and the Christian Jews who came from the Dispersion.

What must be noted here is the meaning of the words "Hebrews" and "Hellenists." The name "Hebrew" is used in only two other places in the New Testament as a reference to Jews. In all three instances it stresses the thoroughly Jewish character of the Jews concerned. A Hebrew was one who in all respects observed the Mosaic law and lived according to the traditions of the fathers. The "Hellenists" were Jews who came out of the Dispersion, with its greater acceptance of Greek ideas. This is indicated by the word "Hellenist" itself: it is derived from the word "Hellas," meaning Greece. The unhappiness between the Hellenists and the Hebrews was therefore a difference between the Christian Jews with a strong Palestinian background and Christian Jews connected with the Dispersion. The Hebrews probably refused full table fellowship with the Hellenists because these did not observe the ceremonial law in its entirety. There may also have been cultural differences between them. This led to inequality in the distribution of food to the poor Hellenist widows, which in turn caused division in the fellowship.

In the non-Christian Hellenist Jewish community there soon developed a surprisingly strong opposition to the church. This is evident from the account of the stoning of Stephen. All his accusers were from the Dispersion: Cyrenians, Alexandrians, Cilicians, and Asians. Those who belonged to the "synagogue of the Freedmen" were probably members of a congregation of Jews who had been returned from captivity outside Palestine by the Romans (Acts 6:8,9). Strange as it may seem, Hellenist rather than Hebrew Jews were the first persecutors of the church. It is probably not an accident that Saul, a Hellenist from Tarsus in Cilicia, held the clothes of those who stoned Stephen. Apparently the Hellenist Jews were more opposed to the church than the Palestinian Jews were. They were therefore probably more hostile to Hellenist Christian Jews than to Hebrew Christian Jews. This may well have led to their attack on Stephen, who seems to have been the leader of the Hellenist Christian Jews in Jerusalem.

The persecution of the church that followed the stoning of Stephen appears not to have extended beyond Jerusalem. The apostles were not molested. The fact that they were not Hellenistic Jews and that they lived the traditional Palestinian Jewish life may account for this. Moreover, the persecution does not seem to have been of long duration.

2. The Proclamation Outside Jerusalem
The departure of many believers from Jerusalem led to

the spread of the gospel. Philip went to Samaria and preached there. This led the church in Jerusalem to send Peter and John to Samaria to inspect the work of Philip there. On their way back to Jerusalem, they preached in many villages of the Samaritans. Philip was called to go to Gaza in southern Palestine. There he met an official from the court of the queen of Ethiopia, a Jewish proselyte who was converted and baptized through his ministry (Acts 8).

Peter went to the coast and preached in Joppa and Caesarea. His visit to these cities resulted in his learning the full meaning of the Pentecost event, namely that Gentiles as well as Jews could become followers of Christ and members of the church (Acts 10:44-48). As a result of this he baptized a non-Jew, Cornelius, a centurion in the Roman army. For this the church in Jerusalem called him to strict account (Acts 11:1-18). Nevertheless, it gladly accepted Peter's report acknowledging that "to the Gentiles also God has granted repentance unto life" (Acts 11:18).

It is clear that the church in Jerusalem exercised a close supervision over the preaching of the gospel outside Jerusalem. We shall see in the next section that it sent Barnabas to Antioch when it heard that the gospel had taken root there (Acts 11:22-24). Some thirteen or fourteen years later it agreed in the well-known council held in Jerusalem that Gentile converts should not be bound by the Mosaic law (Acts 15). It gave the full freedom of the gospel to the Gentiles but it did not use it itself. The results of this attitude soon became clear.

3. Decline of the Palestinian Church

In spite of the preaching of Philip, Peter, John, and others, the gospel did not progress in Palestine. The reason would seem to be that the church in Palestine became a strictly Hebrew church. Apparently the Hellenist element did not return to Jerusalem after the first persecution had ceased. The Hebrew character of the Jerusalem church was so strong that on a later occasion even Peter feared to eat with Gentile Christians in Antioch when brethren from the church in Jerusalem came to visit there (Gal. 2:11-14). As a result it developed no missionary power. It was not possible for the church to be both Christian and Jewish at the same time. Events in Palestine between A.D. 62 and 70 showed how true this was. They almost brought to an end the half-and-half Christianity of the Hebrew church.

The Jewish nation had never forgotten the glory and the kingdom of David, nor the independence it had enjoyed from 142 to 69 B.C., when it came under Roman control. Beginning in the early sixties A.D., the Jews planned revolt against the Romans. Many Jewish leaders advised against such a course, but they were unable to stop it. The Christian Jews had to choose whether or not they would support such a rebellion. They took the side of those who opposed revolt. About the same time, James, the Lord's brother and leader of the church in Jerusalem, was killed. In 66 the Christians decided to leave Jerusalem. They migrated to Pella, a Gentile city across the Jordan, where they remained until after the fall of Jerusalem. They were never again regarded as true Jews. In about A.D. 84, the Jewish leadership in Palestine sent out word to the synagogues everywhere that Christian Jews were to be excluded from their assemblies. A Jewish Christian could therefore no longer both hold his Christian faith and retain his membership in the Jewish community. Soon the church, whose roots were in the Old Testament, whose Savior was a Jew, whose founding apostles were all Jews, whose holy book had been written by Jews, became a fellowship of Gentiles. Even Hellenist Christian Jews began to find themselves strangers in the community that had arisen out of the life and work of the Jewish Messiah.

The unhappy course of Palestinian Christianity may not close our eyes to its great significance in the history of the world church. The beginning of Christianity is inseparably connected with the Jewish church. The first years of the church's life were wholly Jewish years. The first preaching of the gospel among the Gentiles took place through Jewish witnesses. Paul, the father of the Gentile mission, was a Jew and looked to the church in Jerusalem as his highest ecclesiastical and spiritual authority. It was a Jewish church council that made possible full Gentile participation in the life of the church. The church in the world has grown out of the church in Judea. The now wholly Gentile church should never forget the great debt it owes to the wholly Jewish church, which is its mother.

THE CHURCH OUTSIDE PALESTINE

The young man holding the clothes of the Hellenists who

stoned Stephen was a Dispersion Jew named Saul. He was from the city of Tarsus in the Roman province of Cilicia in Asia Minor (today Turkey). He was a strict Pharisee and, at the time of the stoning, probably a student in the school of the great teacher Gamaliel in Jerusalem. Saul was an enemy of the gospel and particularly of the Dispersion or Hellenist Jews who believed in it. In the persecution following the stoning of Stephen, "Saul laid waste the church, and entering house after house, he dragged off men and women and committed them to prison" (Acts 8:3). Some time later, "still breathing threats and murder against the disciples of the Lord," he requested that the Jewish authorities send him to Damascus to persecute believers there. It was on the way to Damascus that the glorified Jesus appeared to him, and Saul became as convinced a disciple of Christ as he had been an enemy (Acts 9:1-31).

1. The Pauline Mission

Thus began the Christian life and missionary career of the man better known to us as Paul, who became the father of the Gentile mission and the author of nearly one-fourth of the New Testament. The thirty years following his conversion were of the greatest importance for the life of the church. In the course of these years, Paul made the following three very significant contributions:

a. On the three extensive missionary journeys Paul made, he established the gospel in Asia Minor, Macedonia, and Greece. Among the churches he founded, Ephesus and Corinth stand out both for their strategic situation and for the length of time Paul labored in them. About twelve years lie between Paul's conversion and his first missionary journey (A.D. 36-48). Except for brief references in Acts and in some of his letters, we know nothing about these "silent years." They were probably spent in evangelistic work in Cilicia and Syria. Acts 15:23,41 and Gal. 1:21 refer to believers and churches in these areas, which may have come out of this earlier work of Paul. A similar uncertainty is associated with Paul's last years. We do know that at the conclusion of his third missionary journey in 57, Paul was arrested in Jerusalem and in 60 was taken to Rome as a prisoner. In 63 he was released, was arrested again in 66, and was killed in the Neronian persecution in 67. While under arrest in Rome between 60 and 63, he was allowed to live in his own house. As a result of his letter to the Romans, his long imprisonment there, and finally his martyrdom in Rome, Paul undoubtedly influenced Christianity in Rome also.

b. The preaching of the gospel began, as we have seen, in a wholly Jewish situation. The first Christians were Jews, and they continued to live and worship like Jews. The main difference between the Christian Jew and the traditional Jew was that the one believed in the Messiah who had come, who had been crucified and raised from the dead; the other believed in a messiah who was still to come. The Christian Jews continued to observe temple worship, circumcision, the Sabbath, and all the other matters of the Mosaic law. When the gospel went to the Gentiles, Jewish Christians expected Gentile believers to receive circumcision before they received baptism. In short, they demanded that Gentiles become Jews before they could become Christians. Paul never accepted this Jewish Christian view of the gospel. He held that Gentile believers could be baptized as Gentiles.

The correctness of Paul's position was put to the test at the end of his first missionary journey. When, on his arrival in Antioch, he reported the conversion of the Gentiles, some Christians came from Jerusalem with the teaching, "Unless you are circumcised according to the custom of Moses, you cannot be saved" (Acts 15:1). This was the important issue that confronted the church. Paul laid the matter before the council of apostles and elders in Jerusalem. After long debate, the council agreed with Paul, but it asked the Gentile believers not to offend Jewish Christians by their conduct with respect to certain Jewish customs (Acts 15:12-21).

The council decision was a great victory for the gospel. It was not, however, a victory that ended the dispute. The disagreement between the Jewish Christians and the Gentile churches lasted until after the fall of Jerusalem to the Romans in A.D. 70. Paul, therefore, did not live to see the full triumph of his missionary theology. Throughout his ministry he was opposed by Jews and Jewish Christians. His letter to the Galatians shows how greatly his work was endangered (Gal. 1:6-9); sometimes he seemed to stand alone. Nevertheless, he persisted to the end. A few years after his death, the breakdown of Jewish Christianity in Palestine and the increasing progress of the gospel outside Palestine removed the Jewish threat. From then on the church pursued its way to gain new victories and to face new enemies.

c. Not least among Paul's contributions to the universal church is his body of letters. Broadly speaking, they are concerned with the *faith* of the church and the *life* of the church. By "faith" we mean the teaching concerning salvation, and by "life" the conduct of those who receive this salvation. Paul's letter to the Romans is concerned with teaching in chapters one through eleven, and with conduct in chapters twelve through sixteen. Paul's first letter to the Corinthians, on the other hand, is chiefly devoted to conduct, while also discussing important teachings like the resurrection and church unity.

Paul's letters have a great deal to say about the risen and exalted Lord. Jesus' example of holy living in a sinful world, however, receives little attention. For this reason it is always necessary to read Paul in the light of the Gospels. Jesus' teaching and example as set forth in the Gospels, and the meaning of Jesus' life, death, and resurrection as set forth in the letters of Paul, must always receive equal emphasis in the church.

2. Egypt, Ethiopia, Syria, and Persia

Luke's account of the early church in Acts gives the impression that the whole movement of Christianity was westward into Europe. This is not a wholly correct impression. There was also an expansion in other directions. Since these are not recorded in the New Testament — or are only referred to in passing — this development is less known than the growth of the church in Europe. This is all the more true because the expansion we wish to note took place in areas that later came under Muslim control. These areas were in the countries known today as Egypt, Syria, Iraq, and Armenia in southern Russia.

It is not known when the gospel reached Egypt. The preacher Apollos, whom we meet in Acts 18 and whom Paul mentions in the first chapter of I Corinthians, was an Alexandrian Jew. We are not informed, however, where he became a disciple. A later report states that it was Mark who first preached the gospel in Egypt and established the church in Alexandria. What we do know is that in the course of the second century Alexandria became a leading center in the Christian church.

As in Egypt, the origin of the church in Ethiopia (Abyssinia) is also unknown. Tradition says that a captive youth from Tyre (in present-day Lebanon) founded it. What seems fairly certain is that, some time in the fourth century, Athanasius, bishop of Alexandria, appointed Frumentius to be the bishop of Axum in what was then northern Abyssinia. In traditional accounts Frumentius is identified as the young man mentioned above.

There is more information about the expansion of the Christian faith in areas north and northeast of Palestine. Already in Acts 9 we learn of believers in Damascus, capital of Syria. About three hundred miles north of Damascus lay Edessa. It was the capital of a small country, Osroeme, situated on the frequently changing border between the Roman and Persian empires. It had trading contacts with Armenia to the north and Syria in the south. Christianity entered in the first part of the second century, probably from Antioch or Damascus, since Edessa like them was Syriac-speaking.

Three hundred miles east of Edessa, across the Tigris, lay Arbela, an old Assyrian city. Converts were made there before the year 100. From these two centers Christianity later radiated into surrounding areas, especially into Armenia. Later we shall have occasion to see how different was the history of these Christian communities — even before the advent of the Muslims — than that of the Christianity of the Roman Empire.

3. Gaul and North Africa

At the beginning of the second century, Christianity had probably been established in Carthage, which was later to play so large a role in the history of the church. It had also entered Gaul (which is modern France), centering especially in the cities of Lyons and Vienne. By the middle of the second century Christianity was spread over a rough rectangle stretching from east to west. Its northern line extended from Arbela to Lyons, and the southern line from Jerusalem via Alexandria to Carthage. Except for Spain, northern Gaul, and Britain, Christianity had been spread empire-wide a hundred years after Jesus' death.

QUESTIONS FOR REVIEW

1. What two aspects in Christ make him a mystery for all who believe in him? Explain.

2. What profound changes did Pentecost cause in the life and worship of the people of God?

3. Describe the difference between the Hebrew and the Hellenist Christians in the Palestinian church.

4. What far-reaching effect did this difference have on the Palestinian church?

5. What is the significance of Paul in the missionary outreach of the church?

6. What are the two major reasons why the eastward expansion of the early church received less attention than the westward expansion.

7. Consulting contemporary maps, indicate in which countries the following early church centers are found today: Alexandria, Antioch, Arbela, Arles, Carthage, Constantinople, Damascus, Ephesus, Edessa, Lyons, Hira, Milan, Nisibus, Rome, Tarsus, Thessalonica?

8. How many of these cities are still in Christian areas? Can you from your general knowledge explain the loss of many early Christian centers?

CHAPTER III

THE LIFE OF THE CHURCH TO 313

Thirty years after the beginning of the church, persecution by the empire replaced persecution by the Jews. It began in A.D. 64 under Nero. The persecution came and went at intervals of varying length, and continued until 313. In that year Emperor Constantine decreed freedom of religion in the empire. During these two and a half centuries of trial the church experienced many changes. Some of these were caused by persecution, others by the growth of the church, doctrinal controversy, or by differences of outlook between the eastern and western sections of the church. Since we will consider these matters in the following chapters, it will be beneficial first to take a good look at the life of the church during this period. How was it governed? How faithfully did it follow the teaching of the New Testament? How did it maintain the high demands of the gospel in the life of its members? If we have some understanding of these aspects of the church's life, we shall have a better idea of what we mean when we speak of "the church" in its various internal and external relationships.

GOVERNMENT

When the church began its life in Jerusalem it was governed by a council of apostles, who guided it in the power and wisdom of the Holy Spirit. That was the government with which the church was born. There were no elders, no deacons, no bishops, no synods, districts, parishes, boards, councils, assemblies, or delegates. Governmental structure and administrative organization developed as the need for these arose. A good example of this is the appointment of the Seven to take care of the needs of the Hellenist widows, reported in the sixth chapter of Acts. They were selected by the church, appointed and ordained by the apostles to meet a specific need.

1. The Office of Elder

Meanwhile, and very early, an office came into being in the church which has remained until the present day. It is the office of elder. It may perhaps be called the basic office of the church. Later offices, notably that of bishop, grew out of or developed in connection with the office of elder. The earliest reference to elders in Acts (11:30) speaks of relief for the poor brethren in Jerusalem, relief sent to the elders there by Barnabas and Saul. In Acts 14:23, Paul and Barnabas are reported to have appointed elders in churches they had established on Paul's first missionary journey. There are various references to elders in the church in later chapters of Acts. Notable among these is chapter 15, which describes the meeting of the Jerusalem council concerning the relations of the Gentiles to the Mosaic law.

How did this office come into being? There is no record of its origin in the New Testament. The very first reference to elders, in Acts 11:29,30, assumes their existence as a known and established fact. It is possible that the separate meetings for worship that the believers in Jerusalem began to hold after Pentecost were patterned after the Jewish synagogue. In the synagogue the elder, who was next to the rulers in authority, occupied a prominent place. It may also be that the older members of the Christian community were automatically looked upon as the leaders, and that later the office of elder became either elective or appointive.

It is concerning the Gentile churches outside Palestine that we read of bishops and deacons. At the beginning of the second century the bishop's office, as we shall see, received an enlarged meaning. Until then, in New Testament use, bishops are called elders and elders are called bishops; the office is one. Paul addressed his Philippian letter to the entire congregation in Philippi, "with the bishops and deacons." In I Timothy 3:1-13, we read of the character qualifications of bishops and deacons; there are none for elders. This would be a strange omission if elders represented a different office than bishops. Particularly is this so when in the same letter we read: "Let the elders who rule well be considered worthy of double honor" (5:17). The identity of elder and bishop is even clearer in Titus 1:5-9, which reads: "This is why I left you in Crete, that you might . . . appoint elders in every town. . . . For a bishop . . . must be blameless. . . ." In each church, therefore, the elders or bishops served as a council of equals, perhaps assisted by deacons, to administer the affairs of the local church.

2. The Bishop

The first clear indication that we have of a difference between elders and bishops is in the letters of Ignatius, bishop of Antioch in Syria, written about A.D. 115. While on his way to Rome as a prisoner—to be put to death because of his Christian witness and leadership—he wrote letters to churches in Asia Minor at Ephesus, Magnesia, Tralles, and Philadelphia, to Polycarp, bishop of Smyrna, and to the church in Rome. In all these letters, except in the letter to Rome, which had no bishop, he called for obedience and loyalty to the local bishop. The office of bishop at the time was that of the leading elder in a congregation or that of the head of all the churches in a city. It was this latter position that Ignatius held in Antioch and Polycarp in Smyrna, and others in Ephesus, Magnesia, Tralles, and Philadelphia. Such bishops were called monarchical bishops ("monarchical" means rule by one). Their office had a remarkable development, as we shall presently note.

The reasons for the rise of the office of monarchical bishop, in distinction from the elder's office, are the following:

a. When a community is governed by a committee or board or council, there is always a tendency for one in the governing group to become the leader. This was especially true in the early church because of its circumstances with respect to administration, persecution, and the rise of heresy.

b. Concerning administration, there was a need to centralize the church's authority. The growth of the church was rapid in many areas, discipline and teaching needed to be well supervised, there were many poor to care for, and there was a need for correspondence between the churches, both near and distant. Such factors invited the rise of a central leader in each significant city or area.

c. The rise of persecution made it necessary for the church to have leaders who could speak and act for the church and her members at all times. Leadership by wise counsel and the example of patience and fearlessness was essential to the church's survival.

d. The appearance of heresy in the church required authoritative leaders to define and uphold the doctrine of the church and to be its spokesmen in doctrinal disputes. The monarchical bishop was not a church dictator. He was in constant touch with his elders and deacons and with the church as a whole in his city or area. As such, he was the representative who was to give leadership in expressing and upholding the common life and faith of the church.

3. The Metropolitan Bishop

It will be helpful in this connection to note the development of the monarchical episcopate, although it will take us beyond the first and second centuries, with which we are concerned in this chapter. In time, the bishop of the church in a capital city of a Roman province came to be regarded as the head of the entire church in that province. He was called the metropolitan bishop (from the Greek word *metropolis,* meaning mother city). In five cities of the empire the metropolitan bishop became known as the patriarch (from the Greek word *patriarches,* meaning first father). The five cities were Rome, Constantinople, Alexandria, Antioch, and after 451, Jerusalem. The patriarch of Rome was the head of the church in the western part of the empire, and he became known as the Pope (from the Latin *papa,* meaning father). From the Reformation on, large sections of the Western church have not recognized the authority of the Pope, but he retains the title.

4. The Office of Deacon

When and how the office of deacon originated is not known. It may well have arisen because of the need the elders felt to obtain help in administering the material affairs of the church. It is, in any case, quite certain that the office did not come into being with the appointment of the Seven mentioned in the sixth chapter of Acts. It is true that the work to which the Seven were appointed is a proper work for deacons. They were not, however, called deacons. There is no record of their continued work in providing for the poor of the congregation. Two of them, Stephen and Philip, receive considerable attention in Acts as preachers of the gospel. In Acts 21:8, Philip is called an evangelist. There is therefore little reason to believe that the office of deacon began with the

Seven. In the time of the Apostolic Fathers deacons ranked third after the bishops and the elders. Ignatius writes that the deacons must "obey the bishop as the grace of God and the board of elders as the law of Jesus Christ." Still later deacons served especially as assistants to the bishops.

5. Temporary and Permanent Offices

Besides the apostles, bishops, elders, and deacons in the early church, there were also men — and some women — with special gifts who gave other leadership in the church. Such were prophets, teachers, pastors, and evangelists. They were generally not associated with a particular church but, like the apostles, were in general service. The *Didache* referred to in the next section gives extensive rules for recognizing and helping traveling prophets and teachers. As these died (as with the apostles), they were not replaced. Believers with special gifts came more and more under the authority of the bishop and performed only local service. The offices of bishop, elder, and deacon became permanent; each had its own responsibilities and authority, and together they formed the continuing government of the church.

DOCTRINE

1. The Apostolic Fathers

At the end of the first century and during the first half of the second century, a significant group of Christian writings appeared in the early church. Their authors are known as the Apostolic Fathers. They were given this name because the church regarded them as disciples of the apostles. The fathers in question, together with the place and date of their writing, are Clement of Rome (A.D. 95), Ignatius of Antioch (110-117), Polycarp of Smyrna (117-118), Barnabas, probably of Alexandria (130), Hermas of Rome (100), and Papias of Hierapolis in Phrygia (140). Included in the writings of these fathers is a handbook of Christian instruction entitled *The Teaching of the Twelve Apostles*, better known as the *Didache* (or teaching), perhaps written in Syria about A.D. 100.

a. The letters of Clement and Polycarp are somewhat similar. They were both written to churches in which there was trouble. A group in the Corinthian church had rebelled against the elders and deposed them. Clement wrote from Rome to plead for the restoration of office to the deposed elders and for unity in the church. In Philippi there was jealousy and disharmony in the church, and Polycarp wrote from Smyrna to help restore the lost unity.

b. The central theme of the letters of Ignatius is the unity of the church and the authority of the bishop. Examples of their advice are: "Pay attention to the bishop and the board of elders and deacons." "Do nothing without the bishop. . . ." "You must all follow the bishop as Jesus Christ followed the Father. . . ." "Let no one do any of the things that have to do with the church without the bishop. . . ."

c. *The Shepherd* of Hermas is the longest of the writings described here. It consists of visions, heavenly commands, and many parables of the Christian life. Its chief concern is repentance that leads to baptism. At baptism all past sins are forgiven. After baptism it is possible to repent of sin and be forgiven only one more time. The sin referred to here is probably major sin, or what in the Roman Catholic Church today would be called mortal sin. Associated with this theme is a constant emphasis on holy living.

d. The letter of Barnabas deals with his understanding of the Old Testament. He turns the whole of the Old Testament into a Christian book by interpreting it figuratively. An example of this is his use of the Old Testament teaching concerning the difference between clean and unclean animals. Animals that chew the cud and have cloven hooves, the Old Testament says, are clean. They are clean *because* they chew the cud and have cloven hooves. Why is this so? Barnabas explains that those who continually think about God's Word and holy things (i.e., those who "chew the cud") and live in this world while at the same time looking forward to the next (i.e., the two parts of the cloven hooves) are pleasing to God (i.e., are clean).

e. *The Didache,* as indicated, is a handbook of Christian teaching that deals with three subjects. The first is the difference between the way of life and the way of death. It describes at some length the way of life by setting forth the manner in which Christians should live. This is sometimes done in pictures that are difficult to forget: "Do not be stretching out your hands to take, and closing them when it comes to giving." The way of death is known by the evil conduct of those who walk in it. Further there are some instructions for Christian worship, and finally interesting indications of how to tell a false prophet from a true one: "Whoever says in the spirit, 'Give me money,' or something else, you shall not listen to him, but if he tells you to give for others who are in want, let no one judge him."

f. Last, and also of least significance, is Papias. All that remain of his writings are some disconnected fragments, thirteen in all, filling about eight pages in an average book. The value of these fragments is chiefly of an historical nature. The second largest is of special interest, however, because of the light it sheds on conceptions early Christians had of the coming reign of Christ: "The days will come when vines will grow each with ten thousand shoots, and ten thousand branches on each shoot, and ten thousand twigs on each branch, and ten thousand clusters on each twig, and ten thousand grapes on each cluster, and each grape when crushed will yield twenty-five jars of wine."

2. Evaluation

One reads these documents with both appreciation and uneasiness. All of them show a deep love for Christ and a high regard for the unity of the church and its fellowship. They also reveal a stern self-discipline intended to maintain holy living and call for a spirit of mutual love among Christians. From these points of view the Apostolic Fathers are edifying reading, and help us to see how deep the spiritual resources of the early church were.

On the other hand, there are teachings that cause concern. Some of the more prominent among these are:

a. *An unhealthy desire for martyrdom.* This is apparent particularly in the letter of Ignatius to the Romans. He begs them to do nothing that will prevent him from being thrown to the lions when he reaches Rome. When he is thrown to them and the lions refuse to attack him, he will force them to do so. "May nothing visible or invisible prevent my reaching the presence of Jesus Christ. Fire and cross and struggles with wild beasts, crushing of bones, mangling of limbs, grinding of my whole body, wicked torments of the devil . . . let them come upon me, only let me reach the presence of Christ." This spirit of *seeking* martyrdom, of glorifying suffering, and the understanding of what is meant by attaining to the presence of Christ were adopted by many Christians during the later persecutions and caused much unnecessary suffering.

b. *The teaching in Hermas'* Shepherd *concerning baptism.* As we have seen, baptism removes all past sins and there can be only one repentance after baptism. This view certainly finds no support in the New Testament. On the contrary, in the New Testament baptism represents the renewal of the heart, new birth, which makes it possible for us to resist sin or to repent of it when we commit it. As a result of this widely believed teaching set forth by Hermas, many believers in the early church refused to be baptized until very late in life or even until they lay on their deathbed. The most notable example of this practice was the emperor Constantine.

c. *An improper emphasis on good works.* Hermas' view of baptism arose out of the belief that sins committed before baptism were done because of ignorance. Therefore they could be forgiven. From that point on the believer himself had to keep his salvation by obedience to God's law. All the Apostolic Fathers place an extremely strong emphasis on law-keeping and good works. In the light of Hermas' teaching on baptism, they often give the impression that the work of salvation is divided into two parts: what Christ has done for us in taking away sins done before baptism, and what we must do after baptism. This was far from Paul's teaching of justification by faith in the saving work of Christ. Paul's teaching of salvation by God's undeserved mercy is an emphasis that is very weak in the Apostolic Fathers. One of the finest statements of salvation by God's undeserved goodness alone is found in Paul's letter to Titus (3:4-7):

> . . . when the goodness and loving kindness of God our Savior appeared, he saved us, not because of deeds done by us in righteousness, but in virtue of his own mercy, by the washing of regeneration and renewal in the Holy Spirit, which he poured out upon us richly through Jesus Christ our Savior, so that we might be justified by his grace and become heirs in hope of eternal life.

The weakening of this teaching in the Apostolic Fathers is a great loss.

d. Barnabas made use of a way of understanding the Bible that was practiced both by Greeks and Jews in their sacred literature. It is called allegorization. This word is derived from the Greek word *allegoria,* meaning the use of an image or figure to describe an entirely different matter than that which the image or figure presents. A proper use of allegory can be an effective way to teach. Hermas uses it a great deal. In a vision which he describes, he saw young men using stones to build a tower standing on water. The tower, we learn, is the church; the young men are angels; the stones are believers; and the water is the water of baptism. Here the same person who uses the figure tells us what the figure means, as, for instance, Jesus did in the parable of the sower. Allegory is wrongly used, however, when a writer or speaker gives meaning to things written or spoken by another who never intended his words to carry that imposed meaning. That is what Barnabas does in the greater part of his letter. The Old Testament writer never intended or dreamt of the meaning Barnabas ascribes to "chewing the cud" and to "cloven hooves." In this way Barnabas made the Old Testament say many things that were never in the mind of Moses and the prophets who spoke in God's name. Barnabas meant to serve the Christian faith, but the way in which he did so is not a good one for us to imitate. Here too a word from Paul is in order: "Do your best to present yourself to God as one approved, a workman who has no need to be ashamed, rightly handling the word of truth" (II Tim. 2:15).

In making these criticisms of the Apostolic Fathers, it is necessary to remember something that is easily forgotten. They stood at the beginning of the history of the church and therefore at the beginning of theological thought. They did not stand where we stand today, with the help of nineteen centuries of reflection on God's Word. It is a question whether we, who notice the shortcomings that have been indicated, would have thought and written more scripturally. If we keep this in mind, we can take humble and fruitful note of the important differences between the New Testament and the Apostolic Fathers.

CONDUCT

1. The Christian in his Community

Christians in the Roman Empire lived their lives very much as Christians do today. They worked on farms, in offices, on ships, in all kinds of trades and employments. They took part in the life of their community, except in those activities that they felt were not in harmony with their religion. This is very clear from the letter written to a certain Diognetus by an unknown Christian, probably some time between A.D. 150 and 180. He sets forth beautifully both the oneness of Christians with the society in which they lived and their difference from it:

> For Christians are not distinguished from the rest of mankind in country or customs. For they do not live somewhere in cities of their own, or use some distinctive language, or practice a peculiar manner of life. Though they . . . follow local customs in dress and food and the rest of their living, their own way of life which they display is wonderful and admittedly strange. . . . They take part in everything like citizens, and endure everything like aliens . . . like everyone else they marry, they have children, but not a common bed . . . they remain on earth, but they are citizens of heaven. . . .

Tertullian, the North African theologian who lived between 150 and 225, gives us a further idea of how Christians differed from their non-Christian neighbors. Writing in his *Apology* (i.e., defense) of the Christian way of life, he describes a worship service. In it money gifts are received, he says, but they are given according to ability: there is no compulsion, all is voluntary. Then he goes on:

> These gifts . . . are not taken and spent on feasts, and drinking bouts and eating houses, but to support and bury poor people, to supply the wants of boys and girls who have no means and parents and of old persons confined now to the house; such, too, as have suffered shipwreck; and if there happen to be any in the mines, or banished to the islands, or shut up in prisons, for nothing but their faithfulness to the cause of God's Church they are cared for by the Christians. It is mainly the deeds of a love so noble that lead many to put a brand on us. "See," they say, "how they love one another." (*Apology*, ch. XXXIX)

2. The Christian and Public Life

It was not, however, always easy to be a Christian in the empire. In many respects Christians could not very well take part in the life of their time. For this they had good reason, but their neighbors did not understand this. Christians would not take part in or even attend public spectacles and amusements because these were often immoral. Many refused service in the army. They questioned whether it was right for a Christian to take part in war, and they felt they could not sacrifice to the emperor as soldiers were required to do. For the same reason Christians could not accept positions in government. Often they were even reluctant to send their children to the common schools because the lessons included instruction in pagan religion. From time to time, as we shall see, these attitudes led to persecution. An example of the difficulties early Christians felt they faced in the empire may be found in the way in which so influential a leader as Tertullian forbade military service:

> We must first inquire whether warfare is proper at all for Christians. . . . Shall the son of peace take part in the battle when it is not fitting for him even to sue at law. . . ? Shall he keep guard before temples which he has renounced. . . ? Then how many other offenses there are involved in the performance of camp offices. . . .

When a pagan soldier becomes a Christian, Tertullian writes, there must be an "immediate abandonment" of military services: if this is not done, he will offend God. The same is true of official positions in the government in general:

> Offices must be either refused, so that we may not fall into acts of sin, or martyrdoms endured that we may get quit of offices.

It must not be thought that all Christians felt and acted as strictly as Tertullian did. It is known that at the end of the second century there were many Christian young men in the Roman armies. Probably there were Christian officials in the many government departments and offices. Nevertheless, there was a definite attitude of separation in these respects that characterized the Christian community as a whole.

3. Marriage and Slavery

In no area was the difference between Christian and pagan so sharp as in the area of marriage. Marriage was strongly protected by the law of monogamy. This was not difficult to do with respect to polygamy, because in the Graeco-Roman world polygamy was not frequent. Concubinage was very common, however, and it was especially against this form of adultery that the church protected marriage. Divorce in the empire was easy to obtain, and here too the church took a very strict position. Many felt that men and women whose marriage partner died should not remarry. It is in view of this that the rendering of the King James Version of I Timothy 3:2,12 and Titus 1:6, to the effect that bishops, elders, and deacons must be "husbands of one wife," has in the Revised Standard Version been changed to read "married only once."

This emphasis on and protection of monogamy and the requirement of continence before marriage did much to uplift the position of women in society. The ancient world had a generally low estimate of womankind. In no area has the gospel been so powerful, so liberating a force as in that of marriage and the home. Polycarp wrote to the Philippians that wives must

> live in the faith that has been given them in love and purity, being devoted to their husbands in all sincerity and loving all alike with perfect chastity and bring up their children in the fear of God.

There is one area of great social importance in which Christianity was slow to act, namely, slavery. There is no open protest against it in the New Testament, and it long remained an acknowledged part of the social structure. However, the position of the slave in the Roman Empire often differed markedly from that of slaves in other areas of the world. Many of the teachers of Roman boys, girls, and older students were educated Greek slaves. The slave could occupy a position of trust in the family, in commerce, and in the government. The Christian slave was honored as an equal in the fellowship of the church. The letter of Paul to Philemon indicates the high regard in which a slave could be held. Nevertheless, there were also among Christians abuses that inevitably attend the ownership of one human being by another. Synods and church councils warned against the improper treatment of slaves.

4. Church Discipline

The conduct of the early Christians was, it is clear, morally strict. The New Testament emphasized holy living.

The Apostolic Fathers taught the gospel as a new law to be obeyed. The Christian faith came to expression in the Roman Empire more in purity of life than in correctness of doctrine. It was particularly on the point of religious and moral purity that the Christian differed from the pagan. The church felt this so strongly that it enforced moral standards with all its power. Therefore, those who broke the accepted laws were sternly disciplined. Hermas taught that there could be only one repentance after baptism. Perhaps this stands in some relationship to Hebrews 10:26,27: "For if we sin deliberately after receiving the knowledge of the truth, there no longer remains a sacrifice for sins, but a fearful prospect of judgment. . . . " (See also Hebrews 6:4-8.) Moreover, John had taught that it was possible to lead a sinless life: "No one who abides in him sins; no one who sins has either seen him or known him" (I John 3:6). At the same time, John writes: "If we say we have no sin, we deceive ourselves, and the truth is not in us" (I John 1:8). Over the years, Jesus' teaching that we must forgive seventy times seven, and John's teaching (I:1:8) have formed the basic attitude of the church. But this was not yet so in the early church. Penance (from the Latin *poenitentia:* punishment) had to prove the genuineness of sorrow for sin before the sinner could receive forgiveness. Therefore, harsh penalties were devised so that on the one hand the sinner might be humbled and thus saved, and on the other hand that the purity of life in the church could be upheld.

The chief means of discipline was public confession or, as the Greek word that was used in this connection meant, "total confession." Tertullian prescribes this fully in his short treatise "Concerning Repentance." In it he fully accepts Hermas' teaching of only one repentance for those who have been baptized. This second repentance is performed thus:

> With regard to the very dress and food, it commands the penitent to lie in sackcloth and ashes, to cover his body in mourning. . . . Moreover, to know no food and drink except such as is plain . . . to bow before the feet of the presbyters and to kneel to God's dear ones. ("On Repentance," ch. IX)

These extreme additions to the requirements of the New Testament long continued to have power. There was protest, especially from the educated and more well-to-do members of the church, but Tertullian answered, "Is it better to be

damned in secret than to be forgiven in public?" From about
the year 100 on, this mode of doing penance was common in
the church. It was doubtless a part of the training that made
the church strong in the face of persecution. We shall also see,
however, that repentance for denying Christ as a result of
persecution became a major problem in the church and contributed greatly to a schism that lasted many years.

Such was the church of the second century. It was a body
of believers that practiced a deep loyalty to its Lord in faith
and in conduct. It gradually gained a definite organization.
Its members lived a life that was at one with the pagan communities in which they lived, but distinct from them in all
practices, laws, and customs that were contrary to their Christian confession. The church needed all its strength of faith,
of organization, and of moral courage to remain true to Christ
in the persecutions that tried to destroy it.

QUESTIONS FOR REVIEW

1. What do we know about the origin of the office of elder
   in the church? How does the New Testament understand the relationship between elder and bishop? What
   did the relationship later become?
2. What do we know about the origin of the office of
   deacon?
3. What were monarchical and metropolitan bishops?
   How did they come to be? Which city in time came to
   have the most influential metropolitan bishop in the
   church?
4. Mention three Apostolic Fathers by name, with their
   writings. What were the chief characteristics of the
   writings of the Apostolic Fathers?
5. Why were Christians reluctant to take part in public
   life? What role did Tertullian play in strengthening
   this view?

6. Compare the early Christian attitudes toward marriage and toward slavery from a Christian point of view.

7. Compare the discipline of your church or denomination with that of the early church.

CHAPTER IV

PERSECUTION IN THE EMPIRE

For more than three hundred years after its birth, the Christian church suffered persecution or was in danger of it. In the course of these three hundred years it also conquered the Roman Empire. The blood of the martyrs, it has been said, is the seed of the church. This is not an empty statement. The persecutions the church suffered in the empire during this time were extremely painful, but they were also extremely fruitful. In the very act of suffering the church was growing. When the persecutions ended, Christianity was established throughout the empire: there was a Christian emperor on the throne, and the position of the church had become so secure that it was no longer dangerous to be a Christian. Indeed, it became disadvantageous, and sometimes dangerous, not to be a Christian. In this chapter we shall note how Christianity became an illegal religion, the accusations against it that caused the persecutions, the defense of the Christians against these accusations, and the extent of the persecutions that took place.

The persecution of the church in the empire may be divided into two main periods. The first extended from the persecutions under the emperor Nero in A.D. 64 to that under Decius in 250; the second period extended from Decius to the end of the persecution under Constantine (313 in the western part of the empire, ten years later in the eastern part). Our concern in this chapter is to understand the persecutions that took place in the first period, from A.D. 64 to 250.

CHRISTIANITY AND THE LAW

We noted in the first chapter the huge extent of the Roman Empire. So large a state could remain united only if it recognized the local customs, tribal laws, and religious convictions and practices of the many peoples it governed. This Rome did as a matter of basic policy. Only in this way could it prevent revolts and secure the loyalty and obedience of the peoples, tribes, and nations that lived in its boundaries.

1. Lawful and Unlawful Religion

With Augustus (in 27 B.C.) the empire began to be governed by one man in whose hands all power was concentrated. It was thus necessary to make his authority as strong and respected as possible. For that purpose, religious veneration of the emperor increased even more the authority he already held through his legal, economic, military, and social power. The Romans gradually began to see their emperor as a god to whom they sacrificed in their temples. This worship became a powerful force in support of the majesty, prestige, and authority of the emperor. It was a religion of ritual: there was no doctrine to be taught or learned, and it was practiced only on official occasions. Emperor worship stood alongside the worship of the ancient gods that men served throughout the empire, and was practiced along with the traditional religions. The state recognized these religions and called such worship *religio licita,* that is, lawful religion.

These religions, rather than the worship of the emperor, sought to meet the daily spiritual needs of the people. Any religion, however, that did not permit the worship of the emperor was considered *religio illicita,* that is, unlawful religion. Only one group of people in the empire did not come under this rule: the Jews were not required to sacrifice to the emperor. There were several reasons for this./ The population of the empire included millions of Jews, and they were not limited to one country or region. They were spread throughout the empire, as noted in the discussion of the Jewish Dispersion in Chapter One. The Jews as a whole were prosperous and well-organized by common bonds of race and religion. They were therefore an influential people. In religion they were monotheists: they considered it sacrilege to worship a god other than the God of their fathers, the creator of the world, the covenant God of Israel. The Roman government was always careful not to offend important elements in the empire. In the matter of sacrifice to the emperor, it could afford to be tolerant with the Jews. They were a very distinct and even separate people in the empire, and few non-Jews became Jews. If the government excused the Jews from sacrificing to the emperor, this would not create serious problems. Nearly all the peoples of the empire were polytheistic in outlook, and polytheistic religion is by its very nature tolerant of other religions. It is true that the Roman government had on more than one occasion made war or conducted police actions against the Jews. However, this was due to Jewish rebellion or other illegal conduct, not Jewish religion.

For thirty years from its beginning, Christianity benefited from the government's attitude toward the Jews. At first only Jews were Christians. When Paul and his co-workers began to take the gospel to the Gentiles, they always began their witness in any city in the local Jewish synagogue. Therefore, Christians stood identified with the Jews both in the public mind and in the view of the government. Even when there were conflicts between Jewish Christians and traditional Jews, the authorities looked upon this as a conflict among Jews. A notable example of this is the effort made by the Jews in Corinth to persuade Gallio, the Roman proconsul of Achaia, to condemn Paul because of his Christian witness. They accused Paul of "persuading men to worship God contrary to the law." To this Gallio replied, " 'If it were a matter of wrongdoing or vicious crime, I should have reason to bear with you, O Jews; but since it is a matter of questions about words and names and your own law, see to it yourselves. I refuse to be a judge of these things. And he drove them from the tribunal" (Acts 18:12-16).

2. *Christianity:* Religio Illicita

As Christianity spread, however, the Jews made it plain to the government that the followers of the Mosaic law and followers of Christ were not one and the same. This was also clear from the fact that Gentiles were becoming Christians in greater numbers than the Jews. In the end, the authorities came to understand the difference between Jew and Christian. Moreover, they came to see that whereas Jews were numerous, wealthy, well-organized, and influential, Christians were few, generally poor, and without influence in society. Their refusal to sacrifice to the emperor therefore caused the government to regard Christianity as *religio illicita,* that is, unlawful religion. From then on Christians risked their goods, their freedom, even their lives to confess the name of Christ. This was the situation in A.D. 64 when Emperor Nero undertook the first persecution of Christians in Rome.

THE CAUSES OF PERSECUTION

The causes for the persecution of the church by the empire were many. Among these, however, one cause was more fundamental than the others. In discussing the causes of persecution, therefore, we must distinguish between the central cause of persecution and additional causes.

1. The Central Cause of Persecution

The basic reason for the persecution of Christians in the Roman Empire was the refusal of the church to permit emperor-worship by its members. Because of this refusal, which in turn occasioned other refusals on the part of the Christians, they were hated, imprisoned, banished to lonely islands, condemned to work as slaves in the mines, cast to the lions as a public spectacle, and executed by the sword. These dreadful punishments did not come to all Christians everywhere and all the time. On the contrary, open persecutions were occasional, in this locality or in that region in the empire. Nevertheless, Christians were always in danger. At any time a mob, a governor of ill will or a persecuting emperor could afflict Christians with a terrible time of suffering.

It was not possible for the church to compromise with the government in this great problem. To worship the emperor meant to agree with polytheism and idolatry. The statue of the emperor at the place of sacrifice was for Christians not a statue but an idol. It pointed to a living or a dead emperor and declared him to be the god who blessed the empire with prosperity in time of peace, with victory in time of war, with the justice of law, the progress of the arts, with fruitfulness of the field, and fertility of the herd. His goodness and power maintained the empire. Moreover, in worshiping the emperor, the Romans did not worship a man named Octavian or Claudius or Hadrian. The emperor, when viewed as a god, was in reality the embodiment of the Roman state. In him the power, the strength, the history, and the glory of the empire were concentrated. Emperor-worship in its deepest meaning was not simply emperor-worship; it was worship of the state. The emperor, who represented the dignity, majesty, and authority of the state, became the state itself.

The refusal of the church to permit emperor-worship

meant that it rejected the state as a god to be worshiped. It could not allow God, the creator of heaven and earth, the father of its Lord, Jesus Christ, to share his glory with a man or with a human institution. It could not do so even if that institution were the powerful imperial Roman state.

On the other hand, the Roman government believed with equal conviction that prosperity in the economy, peace at home, and victory on the frontiers all flowed from the state and its gods. To refuse them worship was to invite their displeasure and vengeance. As a natural result of this conviction, the Romans accused the Christians of being *atheoi,* that is, atheists. The Christians scorned the gods that had made Rome great; they refused to worship the emperor, in whom the state found its human-divine expression. This atheism became the chief accusation against the Christians, and the main cause of their persecution by the Roman state. As we shall see, the Christians' refusal to sacrifice to the emperor did not stand by itself. It had a great deal to do with the attitude of the Christians toward the Roman government, Roman society, and Roman institutions. For this reason it was beyond doubt the central cause of Roman displeasure with the Christians. If the church had been willing to compromise here, there would in all probability have been no persecution.

2. Additional Causes of Persecution

a. In addition to the basic charge that Christians were atheists was the charge that they were also haters of mankind. This charge was supported by a long list of specific accusations. Many Christians, as we have seen, refused service in the army and in the government; they would not attend public spectacles or the theater; and they even refused to send their children to the local schools. Their refusal to sacrifice to the emperor and to the gods, it was said, caused the gods to be displeased, and this brought all manner of calamity on the state. Christians also preached an approaching destruction of the world; their religion broke up families; they mocked the gods of other religions in the empire. Are not people who do such things haters of the society in which they live?

b. Christians were said to be guilty of immoral practices in their religious assemblies. They were believed to eat human flesh, to become drunk, to engage in adultery, and particularly in incest. It is understandable that these charges arose in a hostile society. The Christian communion services were private meetings; Christians often met for purposes of prayer and fellowship at night; Jesus had told his disciples to remember him in the Lord's Supper with the words "this is my body" and "this is my blood"; they drank wine in their communion services, called each other brother and sister, and gave each other a kiss of Christian fellowship in their worship services.

c. Christians were accused of threatening the safety of the state because of their ecclesiastical organization. The fear of revolt made the government distrust parties, unions, and combinations of men everywhere. Therefore it forbade associations of any kind. The church increasingly became organized, with bishops in many of the cities and larger towns. In each congregation there were elders and deacons. District and regional synods were held. In any conflict between the law of the empire and the law of the church the Christians obeyed the law of the church. They called themselves "soldiers of Christ." A government uninformed about Christian language, faith, and practice had reason to be concerned about such developments.

d. Besides these major accusations, there were many lesser ones: the Christian scriptures were self-contradictory; Christianity was young compared with the ancient religions of the empire; Christians regarded Sunday as a holy day and declined to work on it; the resurrection of Jesus was an invention of his disciples; Jesus had been unable to convince his own people of his messianic calling; he was of illegitimate birth; if Jesus were divine, why did he associate with publicans and sinners, live a life of poverty, and die on a cross?

3. *Persecution for the Name of Christ*
As a result of these accusations, Christians were persecuted — not because of what they did but because of what they were. They were Christians; bearing the name of Christ was sufficient cause for persecution. It is in this light that we must read I Peter 4:14-16:

> If you are reproached for the name of Christ, you are blessed, because the spirit of glory and of God rests upon you. But let none of you suffer as a murderer, or a thief, or a wrongdoer, or a mischief-maker; yet if one suffers as a Christian, let him not be ashamed, but under that name let him glorify God.

Persecution because of the name of Christ occurred at the highest levels of government. In a famous exchange of letters between Pliny, the governor of Bithynia in Asia Minor, and the Emperor Trajan in 112, Pliny wrote:

> In investigation of Christians I have never taken part. . . . So I have no little uncertainty whether there is any distinction of age, or whether the very weakest offenders are treated like the stronger . . . whether punishment attaches to the mere name apart from secret crimes, or to the secret crimes connected with the name. Meantime, this is the course I have taken. . . . I asked them whether they were Christians. . . . If they kept to it, I ordered them for execution.

In his reply, Trajan approved of the course that Pliny had followed. However, he ordered that Christians not be hunted out, that if they repented and did sacrifice to the Roman gods they were to be pardoned and set free. In any case, unsigned accusations were not to be admitted.

CHRISTIAN DEFENSE

Our knowledge of the arguments against Christianity comes mainly from a group of Christian writers who are known as the Apologists. In English usage today, the word "apology" generally means an expression of regret for improper speech or action. Originally it meant the defense of a person, cause, institution, or law that was being attacked. An apologist was one who conducted the defense. The Apologists, therefore, were men who defended the Christian cause, mainly in writing.

Between the beginning of the persecutions and A.D. 250 there were many apologists. Writings have come down to us from Christians both in the eastern and the western part of the church: Quadratus, Aristides, Justin Martyr, Tatian, Minucius Felix, Tertullian, Origen, Cyprian, the unknown author of the *Epistle to Diognetus,* and others. Tertullian, Origen, and Cyprian are also known for other writings with which they served the church. The apologies were addressed to emperors, other influential individuals, the Roman Senate, and to the Roman people as a whole. Arguments the Apologists used in their defense of Christianity can be divided into four major groups:

1. Appeal to the authorities to treat Christians justly.
2. Attack on pagan religious beliefs and practices.

3. Presentation of Christian beliefs and way of life.
4. Theological ideas to justify Christianity.

1. The Appeal for Justice

Justin Martyr gives us a good example of the appeal for justice. Roman emperors are called "pious and philosophers, guardians of justice and lovers of learning," and thus they should listen to Christian appeals to be fair and just. He addresses his apology to Emperor Antoninus Pius, his sons, the Roman Senate, and the entire Roman populace. Speaking in behalf of "those of all nations who are unjustly hated," he continues:

> But lest anyone think that this is an unreasonable and reckless utterance, we demand that the charges against the Christians be investigated, and that, if these be substantiated, they be punished as they deserve. . . . But if no one can convict us of anything, true reason forbids you, for the sake of a wicked rumor to wrong blameless men and indeed yourselves, who think fit to direct affairs, not by judgment but by passion . . . it is your business, when you hear us, to be found, as reason demands, good judges. For if, when you have learned the truth, you do not do what is just, you will be before God without excuse. (*First Apology,* III)

He particularly rebuked the authorities for persecuting Christians merely because they had the name "Christian." He pointed out how unjust it is to punish someone not because of any evil that he has done but because he is called by a certain name:

> And those among yourselves who are accused, you do not punish before they are convicted: but in our case you receive the name as proof against us. . . . Again, if any of the accused deny the name, and say that he is not a Christian, you acquit him, as having no evidence against him as a wrongdoer; but if anyone acknowledge that he is a Christian, you punish him on account of this acknowledgement. Justice requires that you inquire into the life both of him who confesses and of him who denies, that by his deeds it may become apparent what kind of man each is. (*First Apology,* IV)

2. The Attack on Pagan Beliefs and Practices

The Apologists replied sharply when the opponents of

Christianity attacked it as superstitious and immoral:

> And neither do we honor with many sacrifices and garlands
> of flowers such deities as men have formed and set in shrines
> and called gods; since we see that these are soulless and dead,
> and have not the form of God . . . but are the names and
> forms of those wicked demons which have appeared.

The men who make these gods are immoral, "skilled in every
vice":

> . . . even their own girls who work along with them they cor-
> rupt. What folly!—that immoral men should be said to fashion
> and make gods for your worship, and that you should appoint
> such men as the guardians of the temples where they are en-
> shrined; not recognizing that it is unlawful even to think or
> say that men are guardians of the gods. (Justin, *First
> Apology,* IX)

Tertullian, writing his *Apology* fifty years after Justin, mocked
the pagan sacrifices and the gods to whom sacrifice was made:

> You offer the worn-out, the scabbed, the corrupting . . . you
> cut off from the fat and the sound the useless parts, such as
> the head and the hoofs, which in your house you would have
> assigned to the slaves or the dogs. . . . Turning to your books
> from which you get your training in wisdom and the nobler
> duties of life, what utterly ridiculous things I find — that for
> Trojans and Greeks the gods fought among themselves like
> pairs of gladiators; that Venus was wounded by a man because
> she would rescue her son Aeneas . . . that Mars was almost
> wasted away by an almost thirteen months' imprisonment . . .
> that Jupiter . . . foully makes love to his own sister. . . .
> (*Apology,* chapter XIV)

3. Presentation of Christian Faith and Practice

The Apologists presented the Christian faith to their readers with dignity and simplicity. The author of the *Epistle to
Diognetus,* writing in about 150, describes the manner in which
the Father sent the Word into the world in this way:

> Did he send him, as a man might think, on a mission of domi-
> nation and fear and terror? Indeed he did not, but in gentle-
> ness and meekness he sent him, as a king sending his own
> son who is himself a king; he sent him as God, he sent him

as man not of forcing; for force is no part of the nature of
God. He sent him as inviting, not pursuing man; he sent him in
love, not in judgment. For he will send him in judgment; and
who shall endure his coming? (*Epistle to Diognetus*, ch. VII)

Tertullian describes the God whom the Christians serve, and
the naturalness of serving him:

> The object of our worship is the one God, he who by his com-
> manding Word, his arranging wisdom, his mighty power,
> brought forth from nothing the entire mass of our world. . . .
> The eye cannot see him, though he is (spiritually) visible. He
> is incomprehensible, though in grace he is manifested. He is
> beyond our utmost thought, though our human faculties con-
> ceive of him. He is therefore equally real and great. . . .
> And this is the crowning guilt of men, that they will not recog-
> nize One, of whom they cannot possibly be ignorant. . . . When-
> ever the soul returns to itself as out of intemperate indulgence,
> or a sleep, or a sickness, and attains something of its natural
> soundness, it speaks of God. . . . "God is great and good" —
> "Which may God give," are the words on every lip. O noble
> testimony of the soul by nature Christian. (*Apology*, XVII)

4. The Use of Theological Argument

Justin Martyr rightly refused to acknowledge that Christianity was a young religion. This argument, he indicated, for-
gets that Christianity is directly related to the Old Testament.
It goes back to Moses, to Abraham, to Adam, to creation. It
is therefore the most ancient of all religions. The Word who
became man in Christ Jesus has been active from the beginning
of the world:

> We have been taught that Christ is the first born of God, and
> we have declared that he is the Word of whom every race of men
> were partakers; and those who lived reasonably were Christians,
> even though they have been thought atheists; as among the
> Greeks Socrates and Heraclitus, and men like them. (*First
> Apology*, XLVI)

> And that you may learn that it was from our teachers (namely
> the Prophets) that Plato borrowed his statement that God . . .
> made the world, hear the very words of Moses. . . . "In the
> beginning God created the heavens and the earth, and the earth
> was invisible and unfurnished, and darkness was upon the face
> of the deep, and the Spirit of God moved over the waters.

And God said, 'Let there be Light,' and it was so." So that both Plato and they who agree with him and we ourselves have learned, and you also can be convinced, that by the Word of God the whole world was made out of the substance spoken of before by Moses. (*First Apology,* LIX)

And that which was said out of the bush to Moses, "I am that I am, the God of Abraham, the God of Isaac, and the God of Jacob, and the God of your fathers," this signifies that they, even though dead, are yet in existence, and are men belonging to Christ himself. (*First Apology,* LXIII)

The theology of Justin was not always correct, as in the statement that Plato learned his philosophy from the Hebrew prophets. But his argument shows an awareness of the unity of all knowledge and its relationship to a common source in God.

It may be doubted that the emperors or leading men in the empire ever read the apologies that were addressed to them. Nevertheless, they served important purposes. They showed that educated men had become followers of Christ and were willing to confess his name openly. They strengthened the faith of the simpler Christians and helped them to answer their critics and persecutors. Not least, they enable us in our day to understand what the church of another time endured, to appreciate freedom of religion where we have it, and to learn that suffering for Christ's sake is not a new thing in the world.

THE EXTENT OF THE PERSECUTIONS

How extensive were the persecutions? Was the church being persecuted continually? Was the severity of persecution equal in all parts of the empire? In answering these questions we must keep in mind two important distinctions. The first is that there was a very great difference between the *official position* of the government on the question of persecution and the *official enforcement* of that position. From about A.D. 100-200 the official position was plain; it was established by Trajan. If a person was accused of being a Christian and he refused to sacrifice to the emperor, he was to be executed. If he sacrificed he was released. Governors were to use their judgment in enforcing the law. In no case should Christians be hunted out.

1. Degrees of Persecution

The official enforcement of this law was quite a different matter. Many local authorities paid little attention to it. There were long periods when Christians were not molested at all. From the beginning of persecution to the time of Decius in 250, all persecution was local. In 202, Septimius Severus forbade conversion to Christianity; Maximinus Thrax (235-238) ordered clergy to be executed. However, their decrees were only partially carried out. Some emperors were neutral in their attitudes toward Christianity, and a few may have been favorably disposed. Between 260 and 305 there was complete rest from persecution. Converts streamed into the churches by the thousands. Under Decius (in 251) and Valerian (257-259) persecution was empire-wide, but it soon came to an end. Under Diocletian and his successors it lasted in the West only briefly, but in the East it did not end until 323. This last period of persecution was the severest of all.

It would thus be quite inaccurate to say that from the time of Nero to that of Constantine the church suffered constant persecution. It is more correct to say that during these two hundred and fifty years there was persecution at various times and with varying degrees of severity. By far the greater part of this time witnessed no open persecution at all.

2. Indirect Persecution

This, however, is not the whole story. Therefore we must note the second important distinction. Persecution can be indirect as well as direct. There are types of persecution other than constant exposure to charges, trial, imprisonment, or death. Christians in the empire were not equals before the law with other citizens. They suffered much from adverse popular opinion against them. They were regarded as haters of mankind, bad citizens, disloyal to the empire. Besides these unfavorable attitudes, they had often to endure unfair administration of justice, discrimination in opportunities to work, and social inequality. In our day of racial, tribal and other kinds of discrimination against minorities, we can grasp an understanding for this kind of persecution. To this

Christians were more or less universally and constantly exposed in the empire until Constantine made Christianity *religio licita*.

QUESTIONS FOR REVIEW

1. Into what two great periods may the persecution of the empire be divided? What are their dates?

2. What was the characteristic feature of the persecution of each period?

3. What did the empire mean by *religio licita* and *religio illicita*? How did Christianity come to move from the first kind of religion to the second?

4. Distinguish between the central cause of persecution and the secondary causes.

5. What did the Romans mean when they accused the Christians of being atheistic, immoral, unpatriotic, haters of mankind?

6. How is the word "apologist" in this chapter related to the word "apology"?

7. Mention three great apologists. When and where did they live, and to whom did they address their writings?

8. Describe briefly each of the four major defenses of Christianity used by the apologists.

9. In what two ways should the word "persecution" be understood in the life of the early church?

CHAPTER V

GNOSTICISM, MARCIONISM, AND MONTANISM

Persecution was a danger the church could easily recognize. It came from outside the church and was practiced by men who openly opposed the gospel. A far more serious threat to the church arose in the second century in the form of teachings that misunderstood the gospel. They appeared in three distinct forms or movements: Gnosticism, the teaching of Marcion, and Montanism. Gnosticism was at first entirely pagan, but in time became associated with Christian teachings. Both Marcion and Montanus were sons of the church and their teachings developed within it. All three held Christ in high esteem. Nevertheless, the Gnostics and Marcion in effect denied the gospel, and Montanus gave a very one-sided view of it. We shall consider each of these teachings in turn.

GNOSTICISM

The world into which the gospel came was deeply concerned with redemption. Philosophy satisfied the minds of intellectuals, but it had no message for the masses. State religion was cold and seemed to be more patriotic than religious in character. Nature religion could not meet the needs of rapidly developing civilization in the empire. For these reasons the mystery religions were popular. They claimed to reveal secret knowledge that provided reconciliation and fellowship with God. In the second century a religious movement related to mystery religion became powerful and gained many adherents. It was known as Gnosticism (from its claim to provide true *gnosis,* i.e., knowledge, about God, man, and redemption). Its root ideas came from the East — India, Babylonia, and Persia — and were similar to fundamental thoughts in Greek philosophy.*

The Gnostic thinkers were deeply impressed by the

*It would be useful at this point to review the section in Chapter One on Greek thought.

Christian religion and especially by its central figure, the redeemer Jesus Christ. They made him and his message a part of their religion. The Gnostics, therefore, brought into being a religion that was a mixture of Eastern, Greek, and Christian ideas. Such a religion is described as syncretistic (from the Greek word *sunkretizein:* to combine, to mix).

1. The Problem of the Gnostics

All Greek and Eastern religions faced a very large and basic problem. They believed that God could not have anything to do with the material world. Evil arises out of matter; God is good. Therefore, he is far removed from all things material. How is it possible that man, who is related to the good God, is also related to evil matter? Who is God? How can we know him? What is man? What is evil? Since God is good, what went wrong in the spiritual world so that its offspring (men) became evil? How can they be redeemed from the evil?

These were the questions that the Gnostics asked. They did not, however, ask them out of intellectual curiosity. Gnostics were not in the first place philosophers. They were deeply concerned with redemption. How can man again have fellowship with God? How can he return to the world of pure spirits? What must be done to achieve release from this material existence? Christianity was a religion of redemption, and there was much in it that the Gnostics could use. Christ the Redeemer was especially attractive to them. He and his work, therefore, became an important part of Gnostic thinking. It was in this way that a Gnosticism composed of Gentile and Christian elements came into being. What did this Gnosticism teach? What was its message of redemption? Why did it threaten the very existence of the gospel?

In trying to answer the questions they asked about God, man, evil, and redemption, the Gnostics accepted one thing as certain. They believed that something must have gone wrong in the spiritual world. That became the starting point of their thinking. Gnosticism provided answers to questions of how it was possible that the spirits of men should fall from their pure spiritual existence and become imprisoned in matter, of what caused their fall, and of what provision was made for their liberation. It provided a *gnosis* (knowledge) concerning the spiritual world, the disharmony that entered it, the restoration of the harmony, and the redemption of men resulting from the restored harmony. This knowledge was *revelation* from the spiritual world and was given to those who were able to receive it. From this secret *gnosis,* Gnosticism took its name.

This *gnosis* was set forth in picture language called myth. We shall first draw the picture and then explain it and report the church's response to it.

2. The Pleroma

Gnosticism begins with belief in a God who originally existed alone. He is variously called the Unknown Father, the Abyss, the Unbegotten. Sometimes he is represented as having a female companion called Silence. He did not desire to remain alone and therefore produced two Aeons (divine beings) called Mind and Truth, male and female respectively. They produced two other couples, World-Life and Man-Church. These, together with the Unknown Father (with or without Silence), made up the *Pleroma,* or Fullness of the divine being. From them the process of multiplication continued. Word-Life produced ten other Aeons, so that there were then eighteen. Man-Church begot twelve Aeons, which made a total of thirty. The Gnostics supported this teaching about thirty Aeons from the New Testament. In the parable of the laborers sent into the vineyard, some were sent the first hour, others the third, still others the sixth, ninth, and eleventh hours. These numbers add up to thirty. Moreover, Jesus began his ministry at the age of thirty. Such an allegorical use of Scripture impressed many Christians as very pious and very profound.

The last Aeon to be born from Man-Church was a female named Wisdom. She had a desire to know the Unknown Father (who in Gnostic teaching is unknowable). Being unable to know him, she became very distressed. In her sorrow — and without the help of her male partner — she produced an offspring named Achamoth (meaning uncertain). Because of her unnatural birth, Achamoth could not remain in the *Pleroma* and fell out of it. When Wisdom saw what she had done, she grieved even more and was utterly comfortless. All the other Aeons grieved with her, and they asked Mind and Truth to help her. These then produced two other Aeons named Christ and Holy Spirit to rescue Wisdom from her sorrow. This they did, and harmony was restored in the *Pleroma*. In gratitude for this, all thirty Aeons together put forth still another Aeon and named him Jesus. These were the events that took place in the *Pleroma;* they also account for the events that took place outside the *Pleroma,* that is, in the world of nature and of men, which we will now consider.

3. *Creation, Evil, and Redemption*

Achamoth produced an offspring named Demiurge (from the Greek, meaning workman, especially the maker of the world, the creator). Achamoth is the mother of all matter. Because of her inferior origin and unworthy character, matter is evil. The Demiurge gave form and shape to this matter; he is therefore the proper creator. From him too come the souls of men. Since the Demiurge is through Achamoth related to Wisdom, she controls him from the *Pleroma,* although he does not know this. Through Wisdom's influence the Demiurge creates men in whom there are good spiritual elements. Wisdom also causes the Aeon Jesus to be born of the virgin Mary. During his lifetime he has revealed this knowledge to men whom he has chosen, and they have passed it on to later generations of good men. At the crucifixion the heavenly Aeon departed from the earthly body in which he had lived, so that the Aeon Jesus was not in fact crucified.

Those who receive this knowledge are elect men, who at death will be freed from the evil matter which includes their bodies. They will then return to the *Pleroma,* from which they received their spiritual existence. All things material are finally surrendered to disorder and destruction.

This, in an extremely simplified form, is the picture language account of the way in which disharmony entered the *Pleroma,* what its results were on the earth, and how the original harmony was finally restored. It was the teaching of the greatest of all the Gnostics, Valentinus, an Alexandrian who taught in Rome and died in about A.D. 160. He was a member of the church, considered himself a Christian, and more than any other Gnostic combined Christian teachings with Greek and oriental ideas.

4. *The Meaning of Gnostic Picture Language*

We must now consider the meaning of the events that took place within and outside the *Pleroma.* The following points may be noted:

a. The eternal Unknown Father is the origin of all spiritual reality.

b. True to Greek and Oriental thinking, he cannot be associated with matter.

c. Nevertheless, since man has a spiritual side to him, there must be some connection between him and the Unknown Father, who is the source of all things spiritual.

d. This connection is provided by the Aeons. Each couple of Aeons is somewhat weaker than the couple before it. The last of the thirty Aeons is Wisdom, who is the weakest of all.

e. Wisdom indirectly became the means for the creation of the world. The creation of the world was not the result of a divine plan but of an accident.

f. This accident or unplanned cause of creation was the desire of Wisdom to know the Unknown Father. It reminds one of the sin of Eve in tempting Adam to eat of the fruit of the tree of the Knowledge of Good and Evil in the Garden of Eden. In Valentinus' account, the sinner was not a human being but an Aeon.

g. The *matter* of the world comes from Achamoth, the unnatural daughter of Wisdom. This explains the evil character of matter.

h. The *form and order* of the world come from Demiurge, the son of Achamoth. From him too come the souls of men.

i. Since Demiurge is somehow controlled by Wisdom, the souls of the men he creates have varying degrees of spirituality; therefore, some of them can be redeemed.

j. The Aeon Wisdom is the connecting link between the wholly spiritual *Pleroma* (which comes out of the Unknown Father) and the material world (which comes out of Achamoth and Demiurge).

k. The connection between the Unknown Father and the evil material world is clearly very weak and distant; but it is still there. Valentinus does not succeed in separating the good God wholly from the origin of evil.

To us the scheme of Valentinus may seem strange and fantastic. To the people of his day it did not seem so. It explained how the world and the people in it came into being, why good is mixed up with evil, where the good and the evil come from, why some people are more spiritual than others, and how redemption may be achieved. He united important

elements in Christianity with the Greek view of the world.
He made it easy for pagans to become Christians and for
Christians to remain pagan. That is what made his teachings
so dangerous, as well as those of other Gnostics (of whom
Irenaeus mentions some fifteen sects).

5. Gnosticism and Christianity

The church therefore rejected Gnosticism, particularly because of the following teachings:

a. Knowledge of and fellowship with the Supreme God is
impossible.

b. The creation of the world is the work of an inferior
deity.

c. The world of matter is evil.

d. The Redeemer is neither God nor man. He did not die
on the cross and was not raised from the dead. He *seemed*
to be human but was not in fact so (the heresy of Docetism,
named from the Greek word *dokein:* to seem).

e. Only some men, those who are spiritual by birth, can
be saved.

f. There is no resurrection.

Gnosticism reached the height of its influence in the
second half of the second century; after that it declined. The
writings of Irenaeus and Tertullian contributed much to its
decline. Gnosticism was very influential in causing far-reaching changes in the church. When it arose there was no strong
church organization. Bishops had local authority only. It was
not clear whether some of the sacred writings in the church had
canonical authority. There was no common statement concerning the doctrine of the church. The three areas of government,
canon of Scripture, and creed were to receive strong development as a result of the Gnostic danger.

MARCIONISM

About A.D. 140 a Christian named Marcion came to Rome
from Sinope, a coastal city in northern Asia Minor. He was
a wealthy ship builder, a deeply religious man, and theologically capable. In Rome he came under the influence of a Gnostic
named Cerdo. According to Irenaeus, Cerdo's chief doctrine
was that

> the God proclaimed by the law and the prophets was not the
> Father of our Lord Jesus Christ. For the former was known,

but the latter was unknown; while the one also was righteous, but the other benevolent. (*Against Heresies*, I, 27:1).

Marcion read both the Old and the New Testaments in the light of this teaching. Its connection with Gnosticism is clear. It also explains his belief that the church was following a religion that was fundamentally Jewish. Marcion is a very good example of the danger of Gnosticism to the church. At the same time, it is not correct simply to call Marcion a Gnostic. This is evident from his doctrine.

1. Old Testament Against New Testament

There was no place in Marcion's theology for the elaborate Gnostic myths about Aeons coming forth from an original divine being. Marcion's entire teaching was based on the Old and the New Testaments. Of these two Testaments, however, he had a peculiar view, which arose from his view of God. The law and the prophets of the Old Testament were for him inspired by the inferior God of whom Cerdo spoke. In the New Testament, on the other hand, Jesus Christ is the revelation of the good Unknown Father.

For Marcion the New Testament does not present a pure teaching about Christ. There are too many Jewish ideas and influences in it. Therefore he made his own New Testament canon. It consisted of the Gospel of Luke and the epistles of Paul, with the exception of those written to Timothy and Titus. He did not accept these writings as they were written, however, but in a substantially edited form. Irenaeus writes:

> . . . he dismembered the Epistles of Paul, removing all that is said by the apostle respecting that God who made the world, to the effect that he is the Father of our Lord Jesus Christ, and also those passages from the prophetical writings which the apostle quotes, in order to teach us that they announced beforehand the coming of the Lord. (*Against Heresies,* I, 27:2)

Similar revision was made in the Gospel of Luke. The reason for Marcion's choice of books for his canon is clear. Paul rejects salvation by the works of the law and emphasizes salvation by grace alone. Marcion distinguished sharply between the inferior God who created the world and gave the law and the God who is the Father of Jesus Christ. The former is just, vengeful, imperfect; he makes mistakes. He teaches an eye for an eye and a tooth for a tooth. The good God, on the other hand, teaches and practices mercy, forgiveness, and love. These two Gods are completely separated in Marcion's teaching, and they are at no point related to each other. Nor does Marcion try to establish any relationship between them. There is an absolute separation between the Old Testament and the New Testament, between the law and the gospel, between Israel and the church. The Old Testament, the law, and Israel come from the Creator-God. The New Testament, the gospel, and the church come from the good God, who is the father of Jesus Christ.

2. Marcion's Christ

Marcion's Christ corresponded to his ideas about God. He appeared suddenly in the fifteenth year of the emperor Tiberius (A.D. 29). He came to reveal the God who until then had been the Unknown Father; his body was not material but appeared to be so; he came directly from heaven and had no human history or parentage. In spite of his good and just life, the Creator-God caused him to be crucified. Since his body was not in fact material (i.e., fleshly), he did not suffer. The Creator-God could not deny that in crucifying the just Christ he had broken his own Old Testament law. To repay this injustice, he gave Christ the souls of those who were to be redeemed. In a certain sense, therefore, Christ purchased their salvation.

Other parts of Marcion's teaching agreed with these views. Matter is evil, and hence Christians should live ascetically. The messiah promised in the Old Testament is still to come. There will be no return of Christ, and there is no resurrection of the dead: life hereafter in fellowship with Christ and the good God is purely spiritual. There is no room for a restoration of the created world.

3. Marcion's Influence

Marcion made it necessary for the church to study the relationship between God the Creator and God the Redeemer. This it did and declared that the Creator and the Redeemer are one and the same God. This God is a God both of love and of justice, and these attributes are revealed in Jesus Christ, in whom the Creator-Redeemer God is incarnate.

Marcion was excommunicated by the Roman Church. He formed his own communion, which had a large following in the second century. It continued on with decreasing numbers until about the seventh century, after which we hear no more about it.

MONTANISM

The movement called Montanism was basically Christian in character. It believed in God the Creator and in Christ the Redeemer according to the faith of the church. In this respect, therefore, it was fundamentally different from both Gnosticism and Marcionism. Nevertheless, it was a religious movement that was not accepted by the church. The reason for this was the manner in which Montanism understood the work of the Holy Spirit.

1. Early History

Montanism arose in Phrygia (central Asia Minor) in A.D. 156. Phrygia was a region known for its wild, prophetic, pagan type of religion. It emphasized "spirit," which was expressed in a condition called ecstasy. The word "ecstasy" literally means to stand outside oneself, that is, a person's acting as though he were not himself. In this condition the pagan priest could fast, suffer pain, dance, see visions, and prophesy. Montanus, after whom the movement is named, had been such a pagan Phrygian priest. On becoming a Christian, he gave up paganism but expressed his new religion in the old religious manner. It was thus natural for him to emphasize the work of the Holy Spirit. The manner in which he made this emphasis set Montanus apart from the Catholic Church. He was joined by two women, Maximilla and Priscilla, who had left their husbands to help him. At first they worked within the Catholic Church, but soon their teachings forced them to establish a separate church organization.

2. Teachings

Montanus taught that through him the age of the Paraclete had come, and that the latter spoke through the prophet Montanus and the two women who helped him. The "new prophecy" was now a reality. Soon the New Jerusalem would descend from heaven and become established in a nearby town named Pepuza. Christians should fast, leave their earthly tasks, and go live in Pepuza to await the end. As Montanism grew, other doctrines and practices were added. One was to marry only once, but abandoning marriage for spiritual reasons was allowed. Every true Christian had to have recognizable spiritual gifts. Martyrdom was to be encouraged, and trying to escape from it was sin. The three leading prophets — Montanus and the two women—could forgive sins, as could others of high spirituality. Women could hold office in the church.

3. Montanism and the Catholic Church

It is understandable that the church leadership opposed Montanism. The emphasis on prophecy and spiritual gifts made many who did not have them wonder whether they were Christians. The forgiveness of sins by the three leaders and by others who had the Spirit in a marked way was very displeasing to the bishops. They wished to keep church discipline in their own hands. The Montanists taught complete separation from the world; the church leaders wanted to keep the church as open as possible to those outside it. In spite of official opposition, however, Montanism spread rapidly. It soon went beyond Asia Minor and entered Europe and North Africa. It was welcomed by many who were being persecuted as a sign of the end. Others accepted it at a time when life in the church was becoming more and more worldly. Montanism was for them a symbol of return to the strictness of the early Christian community. Among these was Tertullian, the great North African theologian, who became a Montanist in about 207.

4. Decline

By that time, some fifty years after Montanus began to preach, Montanism had undergone many changes. The New Jerusalem had not come down to earth at Pepuza. Prophecy had lost much of its urgent character. The early end was still hoped for, but it was no longer a power as it had been at the beginning. Montanus, Maximilla, and Priscilla had died. A Montanist church, with bishops, elders, laws, and organization, had arisen alongside the Catholic Church.

What remained of the early Montanism was a strict Christian life, fasting, separation from the world, confession of Christ in daily life, and willingness to suffer for the faith. This is the kind of Montanist church that Tertullian joined in 207. It established a number of small churches, but it ceased to be a powerful movement. It was not very different from the stricter groups within the Catholic Church; as a result, there did not remain a strong reason for the continued existence of the Montanist church. Gradually its numbers decreased, the later persecution contributed to its decline, and some time between 500 and 550 it disappeared.

5. Influence

Like Gnosticism and Marcionism, Montanism had an effect on the Catholic Church: the church subsequently discouraged prophecy and unusual spiritual powers within it. Discipline became more and more concentrated in the hands of the bishops. Scripture became more fixed as the rule by which the church lived and by which it judged all new movements in its midst. Montanism is, on the one hand, a warning against the abuse of spiritual gifts in the church; on the other hand, it is a call to the church to always leave the way open for the expression of the mind of the Holy Spirit in the church.

QUESTIONS FOR REVIEW

1. Why was mystery religion popular at the time the church was born?

2. What was the redemptive problem to which the Gnostics sought an answer? Why was their answer called Gnosticism (i.e., knowledgeism)?

3. What was the Pleroma, and what happened within it to cause the Gnostic problem?

4. What happened outside the Pleroma as a result of the events that took place within it?

5. Of the eleven points of meaning listed, which three do you consider the most important? Why?

6. What basic teachings of Christianity contradicted the Gnostic faith?

7. In what way was Marcion a Gnostic, and in what way was he not?

8. How did their own native pagan religion influence Montanus and his immediate followers?

9. In what way was Montanism basically Christian in character, and how did it diverge from Christian teaching?

10. Do Gnosticism, Marcionism, and Montanism in some way continue to exist in the Christian church? If so, how?

CHAPTER VI

THE POWER OF THE APOSTOLIC TRADITION

In the course of the second century, the church experienced changes that were not only deep but also permanent. These changes grew out of three emergencies that threatened both the unity and the faith of the church. These three emergencies were the death of the apostles, the appearance of false teachings, and the persecutions. After noting the significance of each of these briefly, we shall at somewhat greater length see how the church responded to them.

a. *The death of the apostles*. After Jesus' return to heaven the apostles were the unquestioned leaders of the church. For three years Jesus had taught them by word and by example. They had witnessed his suffering, his death, his resurrection, and his ascension to heaven. It was to them that Jesus had promised the Holy Spirit and had given the commandment to preach the gospel throughout the world. It was on them and on disciples close to them that the Holy Spirit had descended. After a short time Paul became one of them. They faithfully transmitted the teachings of Jesus in preaching and in writing. They appointed church leaders in local areas. They provided continuity with the earthly life of Jesus. The unity and government of the church arose out of their authority.

By the end of the first century all the apostles had passed away, and many of their disciples were approaching old age. What authority would now take their place? How would the unity of the church be maintained? How would the truth of the gospel be preserved? As the church entered the second century, these were urgent questions.

b. *The appearance of false teachings*. The death of the apostles was not a crisis that stood alone. The further meaning of their departure did not become plain until false teachings arose in the church. Gnosticism, Marcionism, Docetism, and Montanism attracted many in the church. Who could give an answer to these new teachings on behalf of the whole church? Who could speak for the gospel, not only in this city or in that province, but throughout the entire church? This was the second crisis that faced the church.

c. *The persecutions.* The third emergency was the persecution of the church by the empire. What should the church do to meet this trial? How could one section of the church help another section? Who could speak for the church in a persecuted area both to the government and to other parts of the church?

It is clear that the death of the apostles and the rise of false teachings and persecution called for an authority in the church that did not then exist. In the course of the second and third centuries this authority came into being. It came in three distinct forms, all of which, however, were very closely related: the increase of the authority of the bishops; the establishing of the canon of the New Testament; and the development of a creed or statement of faith. It is through these that the early church met the emergencies of its time. The central means by which it did so was the authority of the apostolic tradition.

THE AUTHORITY OF THE BISHOP

We noted earlier (Chapter III) that in about A.D. 100 the office of monarchical bishop was fully in effect. Ignatius (110) speaks of it as a generally recognized office. He refers to the bishops in several churches in Asia Minor. He himself was the bishop of the church in Antioch. His letters urged the churches to whom he wrote to submit to the authority of the bishop. On the other hand, Clement of Rome, writing in about A.D. 95, does not seem to know of such an office. For him bishops and elders were, at least in theory, the same. In all probability he exercised the office of monarchical bishop in Rome without having the title. Clement presents an idea, however, that is not found in Ignatius. In a letter written to the church in Corinth, he speaks of the authority of the elders (or bishops) as being derived from the apostles:

> Christ therefore was sent forth by God, and the Apostles by Christ. . . . Having therefore received their orders . . . they went forth proclaiming that the kingdom of God was at hand. And thus, preaching through countries and cities, they appointed the first-fruits (of their labors), having first proved them by

the Spirit, to be bishops and deacons of those who should afterwards believe. (*First Letter to the Corinthians*, 42)

Clement said nothing about monarchical bishops; what he did say about church officers, however, was perhaps more important than what Ignatius had said. Clement wrote that elders (bishops) and deacons had authority in the church because they followed directly in the line of the apostles. They governed with the authority that Christ had given to the apostles. They were appointed by and spoke with apostolic authority. They had been appointed or ordained by men who had themselves been ordained by the apostles. This teaching is known in the history of church government as apostolic succession.

1. Two Basic Ideas

These two ideas — the centrality of the monarchical bishop (Ignatius) and apostolic succession of office-bearers (Clement of Rome)—were powerfully united in the teaching of a great church father some seventy years later. He was Irenaeus, bishop of Lyons in Gaul, whose anti-Gnostic writings we noted in Chapter V. It was thus in Irenaeus that the authority of the bishop took a tremendous leap forward. Through his teaching the office of bishop not only grew in importance and authority but it had this status and power because the bishop spoke and acted with apostolic authority.

This important teaching of Irenaeus was not simply the result of his thought and study. It arose directly out of his long struggle with Gnosticism. The Gnostics claimed apostolic support for their views. They appealed to secret teachings of Jesus and the apostles which, they said, they had received. It was in response to this claim that Irenaeus replied as follows:

It is within the power of all, therefore, in every church, who may wish to see the truth, to contemplate clearly the tradition of the apostles manifested throughout the whole world; and we are in a position to reckon up those who were by the apostles instituted bishops in the Churches, [and to demonstrate] the succession of these men to our own time. . . . For if the apostles had known hidden mysteries . . . they would have delivered them especially to those to whom they were also committing the churches themselves. For they were desirous that these men be very perfect and blameless in all things, whom also they were leaving behind as their successors, delivering up their own place of government to these men. . . . (*Against Heresies*, III, 3:1)

2. The Importance of Rome

Thus, the bishops were the official interpreters of the gospel. Among them, those bishops who were in charge of churches in which an apostle had served were the most authoritative. Of all these, again, the bishop of Rome as the successor of Peter and Paul was first in rank. Therefore Irenaeus points to

> that tradition derived from the apostles, of the very great, the very ancient, and universally known church founded and organized at Rome by the two most glorious apostles, Peter and Paul; as also [by pointing out] that the faith preached to men comes down to our time by means of the successions of the bishop. For it is a matter of necessity that every church should agree with this church, on account of its pre-eminent authority. . . . (*Against Heresies*, III, 3:2)

At this point Irenaeus mentions all the bishops that have served the church in Rome up to this time. Then he goes on to say:

> . . . Eleutherius does now, in the twelfth place of the apostles, hold the inheritance of the episcopate. In this order and by this succession, the ecclesiastical tradition from the apostles and the preaching of the truth, have come down to us. (*Against Heresies*, III, 3:3)

The remarkable growth of episcopal authority in the course of the second century is clear. Clement of Rome claimed apostolic succession for church officers at the end of the first century. Ignatius, while not speaking of apostolic succession, claimed great authority for the bishop. Irenaeus claimed both apostolic succession and apostolic authority for the bishops of his time and especially for the bishop of Rome. Later the church claimed both apostolic succession and apostolic authority for the Roman bishop by direct descent from St. Peter and further for all those (and only those) bishops and priests who acknowledged the authority of the bishop of Rome. We shall return to this development later. Here we wish to note that as a result of the Gnostic threat to the gospel, the authority of the bishop was greatly increased.

In the middle of the third century, some sixty years after Irenaeus' writings, Cyprian, bishop of Carthage in North

Africa, advanced the bishop's power still further in connection with persecution. Against severe opposition and criticism, he ruled that he alone had the power to determine how those who had denied the faith under persecution and had later repented could be received again into the church. The increase of the power of the bishop, therefore, was one of the ways in which the early church met the dangers that it faced.

THE CANON OF THE NEW TESTAMENT

The death of the apostles had removed the living voice of authority as to what was and what was not the gospel. Their teaching now lived on in spoken and in written tradition. Both the Gnostics and Marcionists appealed to this tradition. About 140, Marcion tried to make the tradition definite. He accepted Paul as the only true apostolic authority. Paul's opposition to the use of the law as a means of salvation fit well with Marcion's teaching, as we have seen. He prepared a New Testament to support his theology. This was the first known attempt to make a New Testament canon. The word "canon" is derived from a Greek word meaning standard or rule. In time canon came to mean the collection of sacred writings by which truth is measured. The fact that Marcion made such a canon is significant. It would seem to indicate that Christians were already then using certain books or letters as authority for the gospel. Indeed, the Apostolic Fathers include many quotations from or references to writings now found in the New Testament. However, there was no collection of Christian writings which, like the Old Testament, was called "Scripture."

1. Early Collections

In the second century such a collection came into being. It was in very large part an answer to the Gnostics, and to Marcion in particular. The collection, which later became the New Testament, grew gradually and in various parts of the church. There were at first, in fact, a number of collections of writings that in time became the single collection now called the New Testament. The order in which the collections appear to have grown is first the Gospels, then Acts and the Pauline epistles, thereupon the general epistles and Revelation. In the course of these developments, most of the present books in the New Testament were accepted by the church as a whole at an early date. Others were accepted in some parts of the church, and held in doubt in other parts. A few books were accepted by some but were finally rejected altogether.

The earliest list of New Testament books of which we have knowledge is contained in the fragment of an ancient manuscript known as the Muratorian Fragment. It was discovered by an Italian scholar named Ludovico Muratori. In 1740 he found the fragment in an eighth-century book of Christian theological literature. This fragment, written in about 170, lists the four Gospels, Ácts, the Pauline epistles, I and II John, Jude, and Revelation. Hebrews, James, the two epistles of Peter, and III John are not included; however, it does include the Apocalypse of Peter, an apocryphal book that was later rejected. Other collections, besides including most of the books in our New Testament, variously include the Shepherd of Hermas, the Epistle of Barnabas, the *Didache,* the Gospel of the Hebrews, the Wisdom of Solomon, and the Acts of Paul.

2. *The Authority of the Canon*
By the year 200 most of the New Testament as we now have it was recognized by the early church as canonical Scripture. The following particulars of the history of the canon should be noted:

a. The most important standard that was applied to determine which books were canonical and which were not was that of *apostolicity*. That is to say, each book had to be written either by an apostle or by one close to an apostle. It is for this reason that the Gospel of Mark (who was associated with Peter) and the Gospel of Luke (who was associated with Paul) were included. For the same reason, decision on Hebrews, James, II Peter, III John, Jude, and Revelation was delayed because of uncertainty about their apostolic authorship. On the other hand, books like the Epistle of Barnabas, the Shepherd of Hermas, the Wisdom of Solomon, and others were rejected because of lack of apostolic connection.

b. It was Athanasius who in the year A.D. 367 first set forth the collection of the New Testament as it presently exists. Two synods, held in Hippo Regius (393) and Carthage (397) in North Africa, under the leadership of Augustine, similarly made the present canon of the New Testament official. The church in both the East and West followed the African example.

c. The canon required nearly three hundred years to grow to completion. This is because the books that were finally approved were accepted by the whole church. The canon did not come into being as a result of the official declaration of Athanasius or of important synods. These official declarations merely confirmed that the church had long accepted these books as God's Word. One may say that both the writing of the books of the New Testament and their acceptance by the church took place under the guidance of the Holy Spirit.

d. In the canon the church had a firm basis for both its faith and its preaching. It came into being because heresy challenged the faith of the church. It was authoritative because it was apostolic in character. It was enduring because the Holy Spirit, speaking through the church in its entirety and over a long period of time, witnessed to its spiritual genuineness and adequacy.

In its need for a new authority after the decease of the apostles, the church sought a clear standard for all men to see. In the case of the authority of the bishops, the standard was their relationship to the apostles by lawful ordination. In the case of the authority of sacred writings, the standard was apostolic authorship or authorship by a writer closely related to one of the apostles. A third way in which the power of the apostolic tradition manifested itself was in the formulation of the first creeds. We must finally consider this last development in the establishing of the triple authority of the early church.

THE APOSTLES' CREED

The English word "creed" is derived from the Latin word *credo,* meaning "I believe." In the language of the church, a creed is a statement of its belief. The oldest creed in common use by the Christian church today is the Apostles' Creed. The apostles did not, in fact, write the Apostles' Creed; it came into being long after their death. It was not written at one time, but gradually grew into its present form. It is called the Apostles' Creed because it faithfully sets forth the central teachings of the apostles. In this section we wish to note first how the Apostles' Creed came into being, and second, why it came into being.

1. Origin of the Apostles' Creed

There are in the New Testament a number of very brief credal statements. They are so short that it is easy to overlook them. They were used in connection with public preaching, baptism, and worship. A few examples are:

> Acts 8:37: "I believe that Jesus Christ is the Son of God."
> Acts 16:31: "Believe in the Lord Jesus, and you will be saved. . . ." Romans 10:9: ". . . if you confess with your lips that Jesus is Lord and believe in your heart that God raised him from the dead, you will be saved."
> I Corinthians 15:3,4: "For I delivered to you as of first importance what I also received, that Christ died for our sins in accordance with the scriptures, that he was buried, that he was raised on the third day in accordance with the scriptures. . . ."
> Philippians 2:10,11: ". . . that at the name of Jesus every knee should bow, in heaven and on earth and under the earth, and every tongue confess that Jesus Christ is Lord, to the glory of God the Father."
> I Timothy 3:16: "He was manifested in the flesh, vindicated in the Spirit, seen by angels, preached among the nations, believed on in the world, taken up in glory."
> II Timothy 2:8: "Remember Jesus Christ, risen from the dead, descended from David. . . ."
> I John 5:1: "Everyone who believes that Jesus is the Christ is a child of God. . . ."

All of these, it should be noted, confess only the Lord Jesus Christ. There is no reference in these confessions of faith to the Father or the Holy Spirit as subjects of confession. In a much smaller group of statements of faith in the New Testament, God or God the Father is also confessed. The most outstanding of these is:

> I Corinthians 8:6: ". . . for us there is one God, the Father, from whom are all things and for whom we exist, and one Lord, Jesus Christ, through whom are all things and through whom we exist."

Other confessions with a double reference are:

> I Timothy 2:5,6: "For there is one God, and there is one mediator between God and men, the man Christ Jesus, who gave himself as a ransom for all. . . ."

I Timothy 6:13-14: "In the presence of God, who gives life to all things, and of Christ Jesus who in his testimony before Pontius Pilate made a good confession, I charge you to keep the commandment unstained and free from reproach until the appearing of our Lord Jesus Christ. . . ."

Finally, a third group includes all the persons of the Trinity. Of these the most outstanding is:

Matthew 28:19: "Go therefore and make disciples of all nations, baptizing them in the name of the Father and of the Son and of the Holy Spirit. . . ."

Further:

II Corinthians 13:14: "The grace of the Lord Jesus Christ and the love of God and the fellowship of the Holy Spirit be with you all."
Ephesians 4:4,5: "There is one body and one Spirit, just as you were called to the one hope that belongs to your call, one Lord, one faith, one baptism, one God and Father of us all, who is above all and through all and in all."

2. Growth of the Apostles' Creed

In these three groups of confessions there is a remarkable progression from the single reference to Christ, to the double reference to God and Christ, and finally to Father, Son, and Holy Spirit. The baptisms recorded in Acts were all done in the name of Jesus only. It is this confession that distinguished Christians from Jews. Belief in God was assumed and was not therefore a matter of special confession. As the gospel spread to the Gentiles, the name of God, especially as Creator, was added. In I Corinthians 8:6, as the context indicates, the addition of God the Father was made in connection with polytheism. Later, the confession to the triune God was made complete by the addition of the Holy Spirit. Meanwhile, the emphasis in enlarging the three parts of the creed was strongly on the second article, namely Jesus Christ. Originally this had been the only article. This aspect has been retained in further developments of the creed. The central and longest part of the Apostles' Creed is that dealing with the Son.

Around the year A.D. 200, the candidate for baptism answered questions before being baptized as follows:

Do you believe in God the Father Almighty?
I believe.
Do you believe in Jesus Christ, the Son of God, who was born of the Holy Spirit and the virgin Mary, who was crucified under Pontius Pilate and died, and rose the third day living from the dead, and ascended into heaven, and sat down at the right hand of the Father, and will come to judge the living and the dead?
I believe.

Do you believe in the Holy Spirit, and the holy Church, and the resurrection of the flesh?
I believe.

This form of questioning the candidate began in Rome. In the course of time, questions were changed into a statement or declaration. The beginning of the Apostles' Creed is found in this development. For a long time the creed that came into being in this way was known as the Roman Creed. As need arose, other beliefs were added. The form in which the Apostles' Creed exists today dates from about the fifth century.

3. *Reasons for the Development of the Apostles' Creed*

The questions that were asked at baptism, as noted above, were a short summary of the instruction previously given to the candidate. The enlargement of these questions and their change into a statement or declaration of faith were occasioned by an important additional reason. The increase in the authority of bishops and the acceptance of certain books as Scripture were not sufficient to refute the Gnostics and other heretics. They claimed to possess secret or apostolic instruction. They also began to use the sacred books to teach their own doctrines. The Roman — later the Apostles' — Creed made this difficult if not impossible. Although the expression "Creator of heaven and earth" was not added to the creed until later, both Irenaeus and Tertullian understand the expression "God the Father Almighty" to mean this. Thus, the Father and the Creator are one and the same. This confession, like the confession that Christ has come in the flesh, was crucified, died, was buried, and rose again on the third day, cut off Gnosticism at the root.

Thus, brief confessions of Christ made at baptism grew into larger confessions. These in turn became questions put to candidates for baptism. Later, questions became statements of faith, and the statements of faith became official creeds. The most important, most universally accepted, and most enduring of the creeds is known as the Apostles' Creed. It states briefly but clearly what the apostles had taught about the Father, the Son, and the Holy Spirit.

4. Conclusion

By the middle of the third century, then, a great change had taken place in the outward form of the church. In the time of the Apostles there was no test of faith other than belief in Jesus Christ as Lord and Savior. The church had been unorganized beyond the local congregation; but the apostles through their knowledge and authority had provided the unity of the church. By 250 there was a firm organization of the church in each main area of the empire, with a bishop at the head of city and district churches. A canon of the New Testament listed the authoritative Scripture. A universally recognized creed taught how Scripture was to be understood. And all this stood fast in apostolic authority: the bishops ruled in apostolic succession; the canon was apostolic writing; and the creed presented the apostolic teaching. It was in this form that the church came out of the struggle with Gnosticism, Marcionism, and Montanism. And it was in this form that it faced the difficult future that lay ahead of it.

QUESTIONS FOR REVIEW

1. What problems were raised by the death of the apostles, the appearance of false teachings, and the rise of persecution?

2. Which two bishops each raised an important idea about the bishop's office in the church? What were these two ideas? Where and when did the bishops who raised them live?

3. Who united these two ideas into a powerful teaching about the bishop's authority? How did this later strengthen the claims of the Roman bishop?

4. What is the meaning of the word "canon"? How is the New Testament canon related to apostolic authority?

5. In what order, and over how long a time, did the canon of the New Testament grow?

6. What is the meaning of the word "creed"? How is this meaning used in commercial transactions today?

7. Since the Apostles' Creed is trinitarian in character (confessing Father, Son, and Holy Spirit), how do you explain that two thirds of it deals with the work of the Son alone?

8. What was the Roman Creed?

9. Outline the way in which questions asked at baptism in time came to form the basic creed of the Christian church.

CHAPTER VII

THREE CITIES: Rome, Carthage, Alexandria

From the beginnings of the early church, its most important centers were found in cities. The first home of the church was in Jerusalem. From there it spread within Palestine to Samaria, Joppa, and Caesarea. Outside Palestine it spread westward from its urban base in Antioch. It found a home in many of the cities of Asia Minor, of which Ephesus was the most important. After crossing the Aegean Sea, its missionaries established churches in Macedonia, Achaia, and Italy, notably in the cities of Philippi, Thessalonica, Corinth, and Rome. Ignatius, on his way to Rome where he was to suffer martyrdom, wrote six of his seven letters to city churches, and the seventh to the bishop of a city church. Somewhat later, in Africa, a flourishing Christianity developed in Alexandria and in Carthage. North and east of Palestine, the main centers were Damascus, Edessa, and Arbela. Thus, in the first centuries Christianity was highly urban in character.

The city character of the Christian church does not necessarily mean that rural areas were neglected. Peter and John, returning from Samaria to Jerusalem, preached the gospel "to many villages of the Samaritans" (Acts 8:25). Paul praised the Christians in Greece because "the word of the Lord sounded forth from you in Macedonia and Achaia," and because their "faith in God has gone forth everywhere" (I Thess. 1:8). Later, the office of rural bishop developed in many areas. The weight of the church's witness and growth, however, was in cities. It was from those centers that the gospel reached out into the surrounding areas.

It was natural for such a city-based religion to produce leading city centers, and this is what happened in the second and third centuries. We have seen that the churches were at first very loosely related to each other; they had a common faith but not a common organization or a common center. The death of the apostles and the rise of heresy and persecution changed this loose relationship into a firmer one. The church developed in four general areas or regions, each with its own ecclesiastical main city: in the West, Rome; in the East, Ephesus; in Egypt, Alexandria; and in North Africa, Carthage. In time, Constantinople overshadowed Ephesus, Alexandria, and Carthage. Antioch in Syria also became a church city of first rank. Jerusalem received the honor of such a position but never had the power. It is sad to note that today, of all these early Christian cities, only Rome remains as a Christian church center. All the others, with the exception of Jerusalem, which is now Jewish, have become Muslim.

During the second and third centuries the three most influential cities in the church were Rome, Carthage, and Alexandria. Each had its own distinct character and made its own distinct contribution to the life of the church. Rome was Latin (Italian) and capital of the empire. Carthage was the leading city of the Roman colony of Africa; of all the western cities in the empire, it was second only to Rome in population and riches. Alexandria was Greek and the intellectual center of the empire. It will be helpful to note briefly the character of the church in each of these important centers.

ROME

In the middle of the third Christian century, the city of Rome was one thousand years old. It was the capital of the largest empire in the history of mankind. The old proverb "all roads lead to Rome" was literally true. Within this great empire, another empire had been planted and had grown large. It was the kingdom of our Lord and Savior Jesus Christ, a kingdom in this world but not of this world. That kingdom did not have an earthly capital, but in important respects it did have an earthly center. This center was the Christian church in the city of Rome. As the years passed, its influence in ecclesiastical and spiritual matters grew ever greater. It was even influential in mundane matters. In 250 the persecuting Roman emperor Decius said that he would rather see a rival emperor in Rome than a Christian bishop. It was to this church that Irenaeus referred as "the most great and universally known church founded and established at Rome by the glorious apostles Peter and Paul." What was it that led both friend and foe to testify so strongly to the power of the Roman church?

1. *Character of the Roman Church*

It is not known exactly when Christianity was introduced in Rome. However, it is believed that by A.D. 49 there was a Christian witness in Rome. Paul wrote his letter to the Romans in 58 or 59. Between 64 and 68, Nero carried out his persecution of the Christians, who were by that time numerous in the city. Both Peter and Paul lost their lives in that persecution. The church, deeply impressed from the beginning by the apostolic tradition, was bound to have high regard for the church in that city where two of her leading apostles were martyred. Even more would this be true when it was remembered that to one of them Jesus had said, "You are Peter, and on this rock I will build my church, and the powers of death shall not prevail against it. I will give you the keys of the kingdom of heaven, and whatever you bind on earth shall be bound in heaven, and whatever you loose on earth shall be loosed in heaven" (Matt. 16:18,19).

The church in Rome was not only Christian; it was also truly Roman. Its members and especially its leaders brought to the service of Christ those qualities of character that had made Rome great. In particular, these qualities were moral discipline, respect for authority, judicial minds, ability at organization, and good practical judgment. The Roman was not inclined to philosophic thought; he was, however, a good judge of clear thinking. He was also good — indeed expert — at keeping diverse groups together. It was this combination of common sense and ability to maintain unity in diversity that gave such long life to the empire. Thus, two things are not surprising: one is that Rome produced no great theologians; the other is that it served again and again as a successful referee in theological disputes between other leading churches.

2. *The Authority of Rome*

The history of the Roman church is in some ways the history of its bishops. This arises from the inseparable relationship that the early church saw between the bishop and apostolic authority. This relationship was doubly meaningful in view of the connection of Peter and Paul with the Roman church. Moreover, the fact that it was situated in the historic capital of the empire gave an additional dignity and prestige to its bishops.

The first indication of the exercise of Rome's spiritual

and ecclesiastical authority over other churches is the letter of Clement of Rome to the church in Corinth in A.D. 95. Although the Roman church did not have an official bishop at that time, Clement was clearly its spokesman. As such, he did not hesitate to rebuke those who had deposed elders in Corinth without good reason (see Chapter III, the section on Doctrine). Some twenty years later, when Ignatius was on his way to Rome to be executed, he looked forward to his martyrdom with great eagerness. In the letter he wrote to the Roman church at that time, he requested them not to prevent his martyrdom. What may well have caused him to write the way he did was his realization of how influential the Roman church was. If it had really wanted to save him from a martyr's death, it would probably have had the power and influence to do so. A further indication of the prestige of Rome is the influence of *The Shepherd,* written by Hermas in about 140. It was an important piece of writing because of its content; but there was another reason for its popularity. Hermas was in all probability a brother of Pius, who was bishop of Rome at that time. This gave additional weight to his book.

3. *The Quartodeciman Controversy*

The strongest early indication of the exercise of Roman authority in the church at large appears in connection with the Easter controversy. This dispute is better known in church history as the Quartodeciman Controversy (the Latin word *quartodecimus* means fourteenth).It concerned the question of the day of the week on which the Lord's death should be commemorated. The debate centered around the difference in the custom followed by the larger part of the church led by Rome and that followed by the churches in Asia Minor led by Ephesus. It is clear from John's Gospel that Jesus was crucified on the Friday of the Jewish Passover week. This Friday is thought to have been the fourteenth day of the month of Nisan, the first month in the Jewish calendar. The church in Asia Minor, influenced in part by Jewish custom, commemorated Christ's death as the Passover Lamb slain for sinners and therefore observed his death on the fourteenth day of the moon — on whatever day of the week that might fall. The rest of the church emphasized the resurrection on the first day of the week, and therefore celebrated Christ's death on the Friday before Easter.

Each section of the church was eager for the other to accept its custom. If both customs were followed, Asia Minor would, once every seven years, be celebrating Christ's death on the same Sunday on which the other churches were commemorating his resurrection. In Rome the problem was particularly urgent. Along with the Roman Christians, there were many Asian Christians constantly living in the city. Thus, Good Friday and Easter would sometimes be observed there on the same day. In 153, Polycarp, bishop of Smyrna, tried to convince the Roman bishop Anicetus to accept the Asian custom. He appealed to the Asian tradition as received from the apostle John; Anicetus pointed to the Roman tradition as received from Peter and Paul. They could not agree, but they parted in good fellowship after Polycarp had administered holy communion as the guest of Anicetus in Rome. Their difference indicated, however, that not every problem could be decided by apostolic example or tradition.

Forty years later, the issue came to much sharper expression. Victor, bishop of Rome, requested Polycrates, bishop of Ephesus, to obtain the consent of all Asian bishops to follow the Roman custom. The Asian bishops, led by Polycrates, refused. Victor had appealed to his apostolic authority. Polycrates appealed to John's apostolic example. In reply, Victor threatened to excommunicate the Asian churches. All sections of the church expressed their displeasure with Victor's aggressive action. Irenaeus wrote to him asking him not to break relations with the Asian churches. Victor did not carry out his threat, but he had given a strong example of Roman authority and Roman claims. In conducting his dispute with the Asian churches, he had gained the support of synods throughout the church, except in Asia Minor. This indicates the power of Rome. At the same time, he could not compel Asia to obey him. Moreover, the dispute showed that the rule of apostolicity was a rule that could not always be applied. Nevertheless, Rome's influence, already great, continued to grow. As our account proceeds, we shall see that in many differences and disputes in the church the judgment of Rome was usually decisive.

CARTHAGE

In the third century A.D., Carthage was the largest and most influential city of the Roman province of Africa. It had a history that was even longer than that of Rome. Carthage had been founded by Phoenician colonists in about 800 B.C. It grew in size and prosperity, subduing the indigenous Berber population. By 270 B.C., the interests of Rome and Carthage were in conflict. This led to the three Punic Wars in which Rome was wholly victorious. In 146, at the end of the last of the wars, Carthage was completely destroyed. During the reign of Caesar Augustus (27 B.C.-A.D. 14) it was organized as a Roman colony, and from that time on it rapidly regained strength and again became a great city. By A.D. 200 it had a population and wealth that were almost the equal of Rome. The population of Carthage and its surrounding area consisted chiefly of three groups: the Berbers, who were mainly farmers and laborers; the Phoenician or Punic element, which formed the middle class; and the Romans, who were the owners of estates and of the leading business enterprises; they formed the upper class. Three languages were spoken: Berber, Punic, and Latin.

1. Growth of the Carthaginian Church

As in the case of Rome, the when and how of Christianity's origins in Carthage and North Africa are not exactly known. Our knowledge of Christianity in Carthage begins at A.D. 180, for by that time a substantial church had come into being there. It existed mainly among the Roman segment of the population, and further among the Punic element that was associated commercially or otherwise with the Romans. Among the remaining Punic segment of the population and among the Berbers the Christian faith was hardly known. Therefore Christianity was not only predominantly urban but also predominantly Latin. The Bible had not been translated into Punic, much less into Berber. Little evangelism was done among the poorer Punic people or among the indigenous Berbers. This is the situation we find when we first meet Carthaginian Christianity. As we shall see, this relationship between Christianity and the people remained characteristic of the North African church.

It is therefore surprising that the Christian population in North Africa was greater than anywhere else in the empire with the exception of Asia Minor. The character of the people had much to do with this. Once converted to Christ, most of them were faithful to the end. The first report that comes to us of the African church is an account of martyrdom. Seven men and five women from the city of Scillium in Numidia, all with Latin names, were executed in Carthage for the sake of the gospel. When Montanism lost strength in Asia Minor, it found a welcome in North Africa. There its special appeal was not its emphasis on the Holy Spirit and on prophecy but rather its practices of self-discipline and asceticism. Its most distinguished follower was Tertullian, the theologian who was mentioned above.

North Africa produced three truly great ecclesiastical figures: Tertullian, who died in 220; Cyprian, who died in 258; and Augustine, who died in 430. Tertullian and Cyprian lived during the period we are now discussing. Augustine we shall meet later.

2. Tertullian

Tertullian was born in Carthage about A.D. 150. His father was a Roman centurion who provided his son with the finest education possible in his day. Tertullian's schooling was in both Greek and Latin. He studied law and became one of the most qualified lawyers in Rome. In about 193 he became a Christian (the circumstances under which he was converted are not known). From that time on he gave himself wholly to the defense and propagation of the gospel. He chose to do this not by direct service in the church but by writing. Because of his strict training at home and his continued self-discipline, he became very sympathetic to Montanism. Its chief appeal for him was its ascetic, world-fleeing character. He was deeply grieved with the unspiritual condition of much of the Christianity around him. This led him finally to leave the Catholic Church and join the Montanist Church. He was a member of it until his death in 220.

Tertullian is remembered exclusively for his writings. They were influential both in his own time and in later times. A number of qualities made him the great religious thinker he was: he was born with a brilliant mind; his life was one of great moral strictness; his conversion was total, leading him to give up a successful career in the Roman legal profession. In its place he became a member of a religious and often persecuted minority, first in the Catholic Church, then in the Montanist Church. His legal training sharpened his natively keen mind, and he mastered Scripture and all the theology that had been written up to his time. He was also a competent philosopher. He knew Roman literature and Roman culture. He wrote and spoke as easily in Greek as in Latin, and his knowledge of history was both full and accurate. He was in every way equipped for his chosen task of defending and propagating the gospel.

Tertullian's writings can be divided into three main groups:

a. *Defense of Christianity:* against Jews, pagans, Gnostics, Marcionites, and the Roman government.

b. *Teaching of Christianity:* doctrinal and ecclesiastical subjects such as baptism, the person of Christ, penitence, the resurrection.

c. *Practice of Christianity:* moral subjects such as virginity, proper dress, monogamy, chastity, fasting, public shows.

The most significant work in the first group is the *Apology,* or defense of Christianity against the persecution of the Roman state. Not only does his sharp legal and theological mind come to the aid of the church here, but he gives a clear picture of the life of both the church and Roman society. Of the works on teaching, Tertullian's most enduring work is his book addressed to Praxeas. In it he indicates what the relationship is between the Father and the Son, a subject that was then much debated. Tertullian's views of this relationship will be noted in Chapter IX.

In works on the practice of Christianity, his views on penitence stand out. He was stern and uncompromising. Quotations from Tertullian in Chapter III say as much about Tertullian as they do about penitence. He saw everything in terms of right or wrong, yes or no, straight or crooked, light or darkness. Therefore, no Christian can become a soldier, no Christian can serve in the government, repentance must be public and humiliating, it is wrong to flee from persecution, there may be only one repentance after baptism. What has Jerusalem, the city of God, to do with Athens, the city of the philosophers? Tertullian was by nature incapable of seeing that Christian duty cannot always be a straight line or a clear choice. Nevertheless, at a time when the church needed courageous example, clear guidance, and loyal obedience to God and his cause, Tertullian spoke mighty words of strength, fearlessness, and wisdom.

3. Cyprian

Cyprian, bishop of Carthage from A.D. 248 to 258, is the second great Carthaginian Christian leader. He was born in about 200 into a wealthy Roman family. Like Tertullian, he enjoyed the best education available, and he too became a lawyer. In 246 he became a Christian and gave himself unreservedly to the service of the church. Two years later the Christian people of Carthage acclaimed him bishop, and an assembly of bishops installed him in office.

Cyprian's rapid rise to first rank in the church caused him much grief during the remaining ten years of his life. Novatus, a leading presbyter, was envious because he had been passed over in favor of a newcomer. He opposed Cyprian on the issue of a problem that soon arose in the North African church. It was the problem of what was to be done with the lapsed, that is, those who denied the Christian faith under persecution. In 250 the persecution under the emperor Decius burst upon the church. It was noted in Chapter IV that the persecutions the church suffered can be divided into two periods: the period of local persecutions from Nero in 64 to Decius in 250, and the period of general persecution throughout the empire — 250 to 313 — which began with Decius and ended with Constantine. Cyprian was bishop of Carthage during the first nine years of this second period.

For more than thirty years there had been no persecution in North Africa; it appeared "safe" to become a Christian. Moreover, Christianity was mainly Roman, and the Romans occupied the positions of wealth and influence. This doubtless led many non-Romans to become church members as a matter of social convenience and professional advancement. In any event, when the persecution began, many denied the Lord whom they had confessed. Every citizen in the empire was required to sacrifice to the gods. When he had done so, he received a *libellus,* or certificate. Anyone who could not show a *libellus* when so required by the government was arrested and put to death if he refused to sacrifice. Some Christians obtained certificates without sacrificing by bribing the authorities who issued them. Others sacrificed to obtain certificates without having been forced to do so. A third group yielded under torture. Finally, there was a fourth group that stood firm. In spite of threats, imprisonment, and torture, they held fast their confession of Christ by refusing to sacrifice. These Christians were known as "confessors." All others who had sacrificed were forbidden to take part in the sacrament of communion.

4. Cyprian's Policies

When the persecution decreased, many repented and applied to be received again into full membership in the church. Cyprian refused. Those who had sacrificed of their own free will or who had done so without being tortured or otherwise compelled could never again receive the sacrament. Since only God could forgive them, they were told to pray to him for forgiveness. The church could help them pastorally, and those who were dying could receive communion if a confessor recommended it. Those who had sacrificed as a result of torture would have to perform a period of penance before being received again. All the others would remain in a state of penitence the rest of their lives.

Cyprian's position caused a storm in the church. Many felt that not even those who had sacrificed under torture ought to be readmitted. Others felt that all who repented should be taken back. Novatus, Cyprian's opponent, joined the lenient party. The confessors supported Novatus. From their prison cells they wrote certificates asking — sometimes even instructing — Cyprian to receive this or that person, or whole groups. Often they did not even know the people whom they were recommending for readmission. Cyprian was also personally criticized because he had gone into hiding when the persecution began. From there he had directed the affairs of the church. He believed that his martyrdom would leave the church leaderless and therefore weaker than if he led it from hiding. He did not follow the path of Ignatius. However, it was in fact more courageous for him to serve the church in hiding than to serve it openly in the city. The church as a whole soon realized this.

In Rome there was a similar problem. The Roman bishop Cornelius supported Cyprian and followed a like policy. One of his presbyters, Novatian (not to be confused with Novatus), who was also a competent theologian, formed a strict party and separated himself and his followers from the Catholic Church. In Carthage, Novatus had had no success in opposing Cyprian; therefore, he went to Rome for support. Not finding support there for his lenient policy, he joined Novatian's party and helped to establish the strict Novatian Church in Carthage. To oppose Cyprian by whatever means seemed more important to Novatus than to remain an honest person.

In 257 a new persecution broke out under the emperor Valerian. The church had now been purified of many nominal members. Cyprian's policy had been supported by the North African bishops and by Rome. When the persecution began again, Cyprian made his policy of readmission more lenient. He declared that all who repented could be received into the church. This action seemed to assure that only the sincerely penitent would apply for readmission. It seemed reasonable to suppose that those who repented for denying Christ in the earlier persecution would have the courage to endure a second persecution.

Another problem that the church had to face at this time concerned the value of baptism administered by ministers in the Novatian Church. Many who had been baptized by the Novatian Church later sought to join the Catholic Church. Cyprian insisted on a second baptism for such applicants, but Rome recognized the Novatian baptism. The Novatian Church, Rome said, is guilty of schism, not of denying the apostolic faith; therefore, its baptism should be recognized. This issue became one of controversy between Rome and Carthage. Renewed persecution in 257, which affected both Africa and Italy, served to postpone a decision on the matter. One hundred fifty years later, with the powerful help of the North African bishop Augustine, the Roman view prevailed.

Finally, Cyprian greatly strengthened the power of the bishops and indirectly the power and influence of Rome. During the persecution under Valerian, Cyprian did not again go into hiding. He felt that the church was now strong enough to lose him if that became necessary. He was soon placed under arrest and confined to his house. Shortly after his arrest he was beheaded, and he joined the long list of martyrs who through their faith, witness, and example continue to call the church to the obedience of Christ.

ALEXANDRIA

In 332 B.C., Alexander the Great had totally destroyed the ancient city of Tyre, Phoenicia's famous seaport, because of its alliance with his enemy Persia. He built another seaport in Egypt to take its place and named it Alexandria. So greatly did it prosper that, as Carthage had become second to Rome in the western part of the empire, Alexandria became second to Rome in the eastern part. Although it was the chief city of Egypt, it was predominantly Greek in character. Among its many beautiful buildings was a museum built by the Ptolemies, which later grew into a university. From 200 B.C. to A.D. 300, Alexandria was the intellectual and cultural center of the Greek world, and in 80 B.C. it came under Roman rule.

Alexandria was also a major center of the Jewish people; more Jews lived there than in any other city in the world. The Septuagint had been translated there in 250 B.C. Also, Philo, the Jewish philosopher, lived and worked there in the first half of the first century. The Jews in Alexandria were Hellenistic Jews: their religion and their attitudes toward life were influenced by Greek thought and practice. As in the case of Rome and Carthage, the date of the beginnings of Christianity in Alexandria are not known. Perhaps Christianity in Egypt, and especially in Alexandria, had received little attention from the leaders of the early church because of the extensive Gnosticism that was found in Alexandria. The two foremost Gnostics, Basilides and Valentinus, were Alexandrians. Our first reliable knowledge of Alexandrian Christianity begins about A.D. 180, the same time that we first hear about Christianity in Carthage. The Alexandrian church produced a number of significant men, two of whom we shall note at this point: Clement and Origen.

1. Clement of Alexandria

Alexandria and Carthage were similar in that both were African cities and had large Christian churches. However, after those similarities, they were in every way different from each other: Carthage was Roman, Alexandria was Greek; Carthage had few Jews, Alexandria numbered its Jews in the tens of thousands; the Carthaginian church was suspicious of culture and learning, the Alexandrian church welcomed them. Carthage, because of its conservatism, was soon to be rent by schism. Alexandria, because of its openness to the Greek world, was soon to produce the early church's greatest heresy. Tertullian placed his stamp on Carthaginian Christianity, Clement placed his on Alexandrian Christianity. To understand Clement and his pupil Origen is to understand Alexandria.

In close connection with the Alexandrian church was a school for Christian instruction that had been founded by a certain Pantaenus. He lectured in his own house and charged no fees, living off the gifts donated by more well-to-do students. The school grew and became known as the Catechetical School (from the Greek, meaning oral instruction). Under Clement, who succeeded Pantaenus as its head in about 190, the school became famous. It endeavored to strengthen the church and to interpret the gospel to educated Greeks.

Clement sought to unite Christianity and Greek philosophy. He taught that the Word (or Logos) of God — namely, his Thought or Reason — has become incarnate in Christ. Before the incarnation, it instructed the whole of humanity, but especially the Jews. The Greeks do not have their wisdom from themselves; they have obtained it in earlier times from the Old Testament. Therefore, they have spoken truth in their philosophy. The knowledge they have gained should be used by Christians to deepen their faith. They would thus come to full knowledge of God. Those who obtain such knowledge would be true gnostics: their *gnosis* would be a combination of simple faith and philosophic understanding. This knowledge would lead to virtue, and virtue to God-likeness. Clement thus attacked the Gnostics with their own name; in a sense, he took the meaning of the Gnostics' name away from them and applied it to Christians. They alone have true knowledge of God, and therefore they alone are true gnostics.

Clement wrote three works focused on the work of the incarnate Logos, Christ Jesus. His first book, *Exhortation to the Heathen*, explains how the Logos first converts us. *The Instructor* shows how the Logos then instructs us. Thirdly, the Logos perfects our knowledge to true *gnosis*, which Clement discusses in his last and longest book, *Miscellanies*. In it he sets forth many rich thoughts, but they do not compose a systematic whole. In Clement's system, the Logos saves by education: he is a teacher and a lawgiver so that we may become immortal; he became a man so that men might learn to become divine.

2. Origen

Origen was born of Christian parents in Alexandria about A.D. 185. As a young man he was known for both his piety of character and brilliance of mind. He attended the Catechetical School and studied under Clement. In 202-203 there was the severe persecution in Alexandria under Emperor Septimius Severus, which scattered the teachers of the Catechetical School. At the age of nineteen, Origen became head of the school because the more mature teachers were not available. With this appointment, he began a life of study, teaching, and writing which lasted to the end of his life. He died in 254 as a result of torture suffered in the Decian persecution.

Origen's writings are many: they include commentaries, devotional essays, a work on Christian doctrine, and an apologetic work. In the apologetic work he quotes and answers the charges against Christianty that had been made in 170 by the pagan writer Celsus. Origen was the first serious student of the text of the Old Testament. He compiled a work known as the *Hexapla* (the Greek word *hexaplous* means sixfold), in which he set forth in six separate columns the original Hebrew text of the Old Testament, the same text in Greek letters to indicate the way in which the Hebrew should be pronounced, and four translations, one of which was the Septuagint. Origen's mind was so productive that he was able to keep six secretaries occupied in writing out the thoughts that he lectured and dictated.

The most significant of all of Origen's writings is his book *Concerning First Principles*. It is a book on Christian doctrine showing clearly his deeply Christian character, his well-trained theological mind, and his Greek way of thinking. We shall note a few of the leading emphases of this book.

One of Origen's most enduring contributions to the theology of the church is his teaching concerning the relationship of God the Son to God the Father. Since this subject will occupy a whole chapter below, we shall note here only that Origen viewed the Son as eternal along with the Father; the Father eternally begets the Son. The well-known teaching of the eternal generation of the Son had its beginning with Origen. What is peculiar in this teaching, however, is the reason Origen gives for it. It is at this point that Origen shows how deeply his Greek background had influenced his theology. The difference between the Creator and the creature, he taught, is so great that it was not appropriate for the Father to create directly. He needed an intermediary to do this for him. That is why the Son had to be generated. It is true that this generation never had a beginning; Father and Son were eternally related as the one who generates and the one who is generated. Nevertheless, Origen's theology has never been able to escape the charge that in it the Son is subordinate to the Father. It is also clear that his teaching about the generation of the Son arose at least in part out of Greek rather than Christian ideas.

3. Origen's Doctrine of Creation

As there was a definite reason for the generation of the Son, so there was a definite reason for the creation of the world. Since God is omnipotent, he must eternally have a world in which to exercise his omnipotence. Therefore, the eternal Son eternally created the world in which the Father could exercise his power. The eternal world the Son created is a world of spirits. In this world all spirits were created equal in glory and in virtue, and all were created with free will. Some of these spirits used this freedom with virtue and nobility; these became angels. Others wholly abused their freedom and became evil; these are now demons. Still a third group were not as obedient as the angels nor as disobedient as the demons; these became men. All of the spirits were created equal, but they became angels, demons, or men through their use of the freedom God gave them. For the angels a heaven has been created, for the demons a hell, and for men this earth. Each group has a home according to its actions in the eternal world of the spirits. Moreover, just as each group has a home according to its merits, so each member of each group has a character and position in life according to his personal merits. Character traits like goodness, kindness, ungratefulness, pride, jealousy, strength, sharpness of mind, generosity, stinginess, and so forth, are all caused by the conduct of their owner in the world of pre-existence. The same is true of conditions like freedom and slavery, riches and poverty, health and sickness. Thus, there is no injustice with God, for he made all men equal in ability, equal in gifts, and equal in freedom. All inequality in life is man's own fault because of conduct in the previous world.

4. Origen's Doctrine of Salvation

It is God's desire, however, to bring men back into fellowship with himself. Therefore, he has given them life on earth in order that through discipline, training, and instruction they may be brought back to him. The Son of God became incarnate in order that he might provide this guidance. But how could the Son, eternally coequal with the Father, become a man? He also needed the help of a mediating spirit. For this reason, the Son of God associated himself with an unfallen spirit from the first, eternal creation. Thereupon this spirit, now one with the Son, went to live in a human body on earth, being born as a child. This child was named Jesus. He suffered, died, and rose again. It was, however, only the human Jesus who suffered and died; the eternal Son of God, who had taken to himself the spirit that became human, did not suffer. This is quite in accordance with the Greek way of thinking that God cannot suffer.

Origen suffered much in his life of nearly seventy years. He was made to feel unwelcome in Alexandria. He was ordained by bishops in Palestine, but this was not recognized in Alexandria and other areas. From 230 he was a guest in other cities, notably in Caesarea. In the Decian persecution he suffered torture, and after his death he was declared a heretic. The church, however, has been greatly helped by his biblical studies. He contributed greatly to destroy Gnosticism. The greatest apology for a church under persecution is Origen's book *Contra Celsus*. In trying to relate Christianity to secular science and philosophy, he made serious mistakes. However, in spite of shortcomings, Origen was the first great theologian of the church. He saw the same God at work in nature and in redemption and tried to relate both to the revelation of God in Christ.

QUESTIONS FOR REVIEW

1. Show that Christianity from its beginning was urban, that is, city-based, in character. How did this carry over to the postapostolic era? Give at least six examples of this development.

2. Why was Rome an influential church center? What was the Quartodeciman Controversy, and how did it contribute to the authority of the church in Rome?

3. Of what racial layers did the people of North Africa consist?

4. What are the names and dates of three great Christian leaders in North Africa? What were the particular services of Tertullian? How did his character and writings both help and hinder the Christian cause?

5. What was Cyprian's policy with respect to the lapsed after persecution? How and why did he change his policy six years later?

6. What was the difference between Novatian and Novatus?

7. How did the question of a second baptism cause a dispute between Rome and Carthage?

8. What are the main points in the history of Alexandria from its beginning to the second century A.D.?

9. Tertullian said, "What has Jerusalem to do with Athens?" What does this mean? Could Clement of Alexandria have made such a statement? Why?

10. In which way does Origen's doctrine of the eternal generation of the Son reveal his Greek way of thinking? What were his views of creation and salvation?

CHAPTER VIII

DIOCLETIAN AND CONSTANTINE

In this chapter we reach the climax in the history of church-state relations in the Roman Empire. We shall meet the last of the great pagan emperors — Diocletian — and the first of the Christian emperors — Constantine. This profound change did not take place without a final ordeal that tried the church's faith. The great persecution initiated by Diocletian introduced the change from the old order to the new. We must take note of these two men and of the church's dark hour of trial which lies between them.

DIOCLETIAN

Before we can measure the significance of Diocletian, we must first note the conditions that existed in the empire during the one hundred years that preceded him. Diocletian became emperor in 284. The last of the famous Roman emperors before him was Marcus Aurelius, who died in 180. The Golden Age of Rome that had begun with Augustus in 27 B.C. came to an end with Aurelius. During the two hundred years from Augustus to Aurelius, Rome had enjoyed peace, except for some military activity at the frontiers. There had been no civil war; the economy had prospered; literature and the arts had flourished; and Roman law had governed the peoples of the empire from Britain in the far west to Arabia in the far east. However, peace, prosperity, and security had brought ease, loose morals, and decreasing respect for authority. The qualities of character that had made Rome great began to weaken.

1. Condition of the Empire
This weakening was most evident in the army, on which the stability of the empire mainly depended. Already in the second century, young men from good families began to lose interest in military careers. This trend became stronger in the

third century. The government was increasingly forced to recruit soldiers among noncitizens in the empire and even among the German tribes outside the empire. Before long, the army and its officers consisted to a large extent of mercenaries; to them, self-interest was greater than loyalty in serving the empire. Furthermore, the army soon became the chief political power in the empire. The emperor was no longer chosen by the senate; the army chose generals to be emperors. From A.D. 180 to 284 emperors were prisoners of the army, and an emperor who did not please the army was killed. If he was too strict, or if he was not strict enough, if he wanted to do battle when the soldiers did not, if he did not pay enough, if the army did not like his policy in this or that matter, he was murdered and another general appointed in his place — whether the new one liked it or not. From 180 to 284 Rome had twenty-five emperors. In the two hundred years from Augustus to Aurelius there had been only thirteen.* Of the twenty-five who reigned between 180 and 284, twenty-one were murdered; one was betrayed in battle by one of his generals; another was taken prisoner by the Persians and never heard of again; and only two died natural deaths.

The instability and disorder in the empire was soon noticed by the tribes at the borders. They crossed the Rhine and the Danube by the thousands to settle in the empire. The Persians made war in the east. In Syria and in Gaul, independent kingdoms arose to maintain local order. These developments led to heavier taxation to repel invaders and to maintain authority in the empire. As a result of this taxation, economic life broke down: trade became more local and less empire-wide. Farms became less productive because the fruits of hard work were eaten up by taxes. Everywhere people and authorities feared the soldiers, who took whatever they liked. Money lost value because the government mixed cheap metals into gold and silver coins. The rich became poor, and the poor had no hope. Such was the situation in the Roman Empire when Diocletian became emperor.

Diocletian was not a brilliant man, but he had character and the courage that is inherent in true character. He was not

*This number does not include the three emperors Galba, Otho, and Vitellius, who in A.D. 69 fought for the crown in the abnormal situation following the death of Nero. All three died in the struggle.

a traditional Roman but an Illyrian (Illyria, also called Dal-matia, constituted the western part of what is today Yugo-slavia). Four of his fellow-countrymen had been emperor be-fore him: Claudius II (268-270), Aurelian (270-275), Probus (276-282), and Carus (282-283). All were capable and fearless men, but their virtue was not rewarded. Only Claudius died a natural death. Aurelian, called "the restorer of the world" because of his efforts to reform the government, was murdered by a group of officers; Probus was killed when he put his army to the peaceful work of digging a canal; the cause of Carus' death is not certain, but murder was suspected.

2. Reorganization of the Government

When Diocletian became emperor, therefore, he was fully aware of the difficulty of his task. He also understood the personal danger to which he was exposed. However, he had one great advantage. The danger to the empire was now so great that people everywhere were looking for an emperor-savior. Even the army was willing to surrender some of its lawless power. Diocletian proved to be the right man in the right place at the right time. His greatest contribution was the administrative reform of the empire. He saw that the empire was too large to be governed by one man, and hence he di-vided it into two parts — the West and the East. The dividing line ran through the Adriatic Sea between Italy and Illyria. Each half was governed by an Augustus (i.e., an emperor), who after some years was assisted by a Caesar. The Caesar was to succeed the Augustus at his retirement or at his death. Each of the four had a capital, an army, a court, and a section of the empire to rule. Diocletian became Augustus in the East; Maximian, an Illyrian general, became Augustus in the West. Galerius, Diocletian's son-in-law, became his Caesar; Maxim-ian's Caesar was Constantius. Galerius was a Thracian, Con-stantius an Illyrian; both were highly capable military men.

Although Diocletian and Maximian were both Augustus, Diocletian remained supreme. He not only retained final and supreme power, but he also ruled in the East, the most de-veloped and cultured part of the empire. He and Maximian no longer asked advice from or consulted with the senate, through whom the earlier emperors had governed; they ruled alone. Diocletian lived in a splendid palace. He followed the ways of Persian monarchs in dress and court routine. Any who had an interview with him had to fall prostrate before him and kiss the hem of his robe. He ceased to be the *Princeps,* or leading citizen of the empire, as the first Augustus and his successors had been; he became "lord and god," and all that surrounded him was sacred and divine. The worship of the emperor was now complete. The reason for this new lifestyle was in part a very practical one. It made it more difficult for potential assassins to carry out an attack on his person.

We have seen two fundamental changes that Diocletian introduced. First, the empire was divided among two Augusti and two Caesars, with final power in the hands of Diocletian. Second, he ascribed divinity to the person of the emperor in order to make his life more secure and, no doubt, his authority weightier. A further change must be noted, perhaps the most significant of all. Under the earlier emperors, local custom, local tradition, and local government had been greatly respected. The army had protected the empire and provided safety within it, but it had not governed the empire. Under Diocletian the army tripled in size and set up a complete military government. Civilian government agencies became servants of the army. Dishonesty became universal, freedom decreased everywhere, and government by the army was often incompetent.

Moreover, the historic city of Rome ceased to be the capital of the empire. No Augustus or Caesar lived there. The capitals in which they lived were determined by military needs. From Nicomedia in Asia Minor, Diocletian controlled the eastern Danube and the Persian frontiers. Galerius governed the western Danube border from Sirmium in northern Illyria. From Milan in northern Italy, Maximian kept an eye on the tribes to the north of the Italian border. Constantius kept watch on the Rhine and on the Germans east of it from Treves (now Trier) in northeastern Gaul. However, the government's abandonment of Rome indirectly strengthened the power and prestige of the Roman Church and its bishop. The history, the tradition, the glory and fame of the city of Rome did not die when government headquarters moved elsewhere. Under the later emperors, the bishop of Rome became the foremost official person in the ancient city.

3. Results of Diocletian's Reorganization

For twenty-one years Diocletian gave himself to the reform of the imperial government. During these two decades the empire regathered its strength, fought back the barbarians, held firm at the frontiers, and gained a new self-respect. In this way Rome survived its crisis of military rule in the third century. But it paid a heavy price for survival: it regained its security, but the price it paid was economic decline and the loss of local freedoms out of which the empire had grown. The loss was greatest in the West. There the empire ceased to exist in 476. In the East it lasted a thousand years longer until the fall of Constantinople in 1453 to the Muslims.

THE DARKEST HOUR

In considering the last persecution of the church before the time of Constantine, it will be useful to briefly review the history of the persecution of Christians in the Roman Empire. As we noted above, the persecutions as a whole can be divided into two periods. During the first, extending up to 250, the persecution was local; in the second, after 250, persecutions were empire-wide.

1. Review of Persecution: First Period

The first period begins with Nero. During his reign, in A.D. 64, there was a severe persecution in Rome. A similarly local but less severe persecution took place under Domitian in 95. From Trajan, who began to reign in 98, to the end of the reign of Antoninus Pius (160), Christianity was both in danger and, in a certain sense, under protection. It was a *religio illicita* and therefore exposed to persecution. But it was also protected: Trajan had forbidden legal action on anonymous accusations. Hadrian forbade condemnation of Christians without evidence. Moreover, he had ordered that Christians were not to be sought out. In this situation there was limited persecution, but the church grew greatly in spite of it. Marcus Aurelius (160-180) was more aggressive. He actively opposed Christianity, and under him a very severe persecution occurred in Gaul in 177. From 180 to 250 Christianity remained *religio illicita,* but little was done about it. Indeed, Christianity flourished in the empire during these seventy years. The chief exception in this long period of quiet was a severe persecution under the emperor Septimius Severus in 202 and 203, mainly in Egypt and Carthage. He prohibited conversion from paganism

56233

to Christianity. The public confession of Christ at baptism, therefore, was a dangerous act. He also persecuted the clergy, which is evident from the scattering of the teachers of the Catechetical School in Alexandria. Briefer and less serious persecutions took place under Caracalla in North Africa and under Maximin Thrax in Asia Minor and Palestine. They brought to an end the persecutions in the first period.

2. Review of Persecution: Second Period

During the second period, persecution was not local but general throughout the empire. It was occasioned in varying degrees by five causes: first, the remarkable growth of the Christian church; second, the sharp decline in the economic and moral life of the empire; third, the approaching one thousandth anniversary of the founding of Rome; fourth, the view of many leading Romans that the church was a state within the state and was therefore a danger to the empire; and fifth, arising from the foregoing, the fear that Rome's decline was due to the displeasure of the gods with the progress of Christianity.

In this second period there were three great persecutions. The first was under Decius between 250 and 253. It caused more apostasy in the church than had any previous persecution. The second persecution occurred under Valerian in 257. It aimed to destroy the Christian leadership by forcing the clergy and leading Christians in the government and society to recant, and by killing those who refused. It was in this persecution that Cyprian was executed in Carthage and Bishop Sixtus II in Rome. Valerian was taken prisoner in a war with the Persians, and his son Gallienus cancelled the persecution. In doing so he in effect cancelled the legal status of Christianity as *religio illicita*. His edict of toleration was addressed "to the bishops." It restored places of worship and cemeteries to the churches as organized bodies.

The Valerian persecution was followed by forty-three years of peace. During these years Christianity grew as never before. The edict of toleration published by Gallienus led Christians to believe that persecution had come to an end permanently. Beautiful churches were built, and many people of influence and education became Christians. At the same time the economic, military, and social situation in the empire became more and more alarming. The capture of Valerian by the Persians, and the rise of independent kingdoms in Syria and in Gaul, were symbols of the weakened condition to which the empire had fallen. From 260 to 305, a line of capable emperors labored to restore order and strength to the empire. Diocletian was the last and greatest of these.

3. The Diocletian Persecution

It is therefore painful to record that in 303 Diocletian became a persecutor. In that year, two years before he abdicated as Augustus, he initiated the third, the longest and most horrible of the three persecutions in the second period. It is difficult to understand Diocletian's action. His wife Prisca and his daughter Valeria had become Christians; many servants and officials in the imperial palace were Christians. For twenty years he had shown no desire to persecute the church. Thus, it is generally believed that the person most responsible for the persecution was Galerius, Diocletian's Caesar. It is known that he hated Christianity. His mother, a worshipper of the pagan god Cybele, urged him to persecute. It may well be that Diocletian found it impossible to give a good Roman answer to the five reasons for persecution listed above. He therefore yielded to the urgings of Galerius, but on the condition that Christians not be killed. Nevertheless, it was Diocletian who authorized the persecution. It began in his reign and he must bear the official responsibility for it.

The persecution began on February 23, 303, without any warning. On that day police and workmen went to the big church in Nicomedia, Diocletian's capital, burned its Bibles, took its furnishings, and destroyed the building totally. During the year that followed, four edicts of persecution were published. These edicts successively declared that:

1. All Christians of the upper classes would be deprived of their official positions and privileges. Christians in the imperial court would become slaves unless they renounced Christianity. All Christians were deprived of their rights of citizenship. All churches were to be destroyed, and all sacred books burned.

2. All Christian clergy and church officials were to be imprisoned. Eusebius, in his *History of the Church,* writes:

> In every town great numbers were locked up, and everywhere the prisons which had been built long before for murderers and grave-robbers were crowded with bishops, presbyters

and deacons, readers and exorcists, so that now there was no room in them for those convicted of crimes. (Bk. 8, par. 6)

3. All leaders so imprisoned were to be compelled either to sacrifice to the gods or to be "mutilated by endless tortures."

4. The fourth decree required all Christians, without exception, to sacrifice to the gods on pain of imprisonment or severer punishment.

The Diocletian persecution lasted ten years. It was not pursued strongly in the West, where neither Constantius nor his son Constantine were sympathetic to it. But in the areas governed by Diocletian and Galerius the persecution was very severe. Diocletian resigned the emperor's office in 305, as did Maximian in the West. And although Galerius was the main persecutor, in church history the persecution has retained the name of the emperor who initiated it.

The persecution was utterly severe. At its end, if a church leader did not have the marks of the whip or of other forms of torture on his body, he was suspected of having betrayed the faith. Thousands died and thousands more went through life maimed, blinded, or disfigured by torture. In 311, Galerius became seriously ill. After an eight-year effort to destroy the church, he found it stronger and more determined than at the beginning. His sickness brought him near death. Eusebius writes: "As he struggled with this terrible sickness, he was filled with remorse for his cruel treatment of God's servants. So he pulled himself together, and after first making open confession to the God of the universe, he called his court officials and ordered them to lose no time in stopping the persecution of Christians." The edict of toleration which he published concluded as follows:

So in view of our benevolence and the established custom by which we invariably grant pardon to all men, we have thought it proper in this matter also to extend our clemency most gladly, so that Christians may again exist and rebuild the houses in which they used to meet, on condition that they do nothing contrary to public order. . . . Therefore, in view of this our clemency, they are in duty bound to beseech their own god for our security, and that of the state and of themselves, in order that in every way the state may be preserved in health and they may be able to live free from anxiety in their own homes. (Bk. 8, par. 17)

Five days later Galerius died. He was succeeded by his Caesar, Maximin Daia, who reinstituted the persecution after six months. But he was also unable to maintain it. Political pressure and civil war forced him to publish an edict of toleration. It read in part as follows:

> In order, then, to remove all doubt, we publish this decree, that it may be plain to all, that such as wish to follow this sect and worship (Christianity) are at liberty to do so — namely to adopt and practice this religion. They are also allowed to build Lord's Houses (churches), and if houses or lands belonging to the Christians have been confiscated . . . they shall be restored to them. (Eusebius, Bk. 9, par. 10)

Three months later Maximin Daia was dead.

Diocletian's end was as unhappy as that of Galerius and Maximin. When he published the decree to persecute in 303, he required his wife and daughter to sacrifice. From 305 on he lived in retirement in a beautiful palace in Spalato, Illyria. After the death of Galerius in 311, Maximin banished Diocletian's wife Prisca to one place, and his daughter Valeria, wife of Galerius, to another. When Maximin was defeated in the civil war of 313, Prisca and Valeria were captured and killed. In all this Diocletian was powerless to change the course of events. The persecution had been a failure, his wife and daughter and son-in-law were dead, and the empire he had ruled so long was in the hands of others. He died in great loneliness and bitterness of spirit in December 316.

CONSTANTINE

Constantine was born in about A.D. 288. His father was Constantius, the Illyrian general in the Roman army who in 293 became the Caesar of Maximian, the Augustus in the West. In 305, Maximian and Diocletian abdicated; Constantius then became Augustus in the West, and Galerius in the East. At that time Constantine was living at the court of Galerius; it appears that he was there as a hostage to guarantee the loyalty of Constantius.

1. Constantine Becomes Emperor

In 306, Constantius became seriously ill in the town of Boulogne in northwestern Gaul. On hearing this, Constantine left Galerius' court without permission to visit his father.

A few months later, Constantius died and his soldiers proclaimed Constantine his successor. With this there began a confusing struggle for imperial power. Constantine married Fausta, the daughter of Maximian, who had just abdicated along with Diocletian. Soon, however, Maxentius, the son of Maximian, tried to gain control of the West. In 308, with the support of his father, he declared himself to be the Augustus of the western empire. Constantine took Maximian prisoner and permitted him to commit suicide. Meanwhile he had secured the loyalty and support of all the Roman armies in Britain and in Gaul. He was now ready to meet Maxentius in Italy.

In 312, Constantine marched into Italy to remove Maxentius from his position of power in Rome. The two armies faced each other a few miles outside the city. The day before the battle Constantine saw the sign of a cross in the sky and above it the words *In hoc signo vinces* (in this sign conquer). Constantine pledged that if he won the battle he would become a Christian. The next day, October 28, his army won a complete victory, and Maxentius was drowned as he tried to escape across the Tiber River. The seven years between 305 and 312, therefore, were extremely significant both for the empire and for Constantine. Maximian had abdicated; his successor Constantius had died; Maximian later killed himself, and his son Maxentius was dead after military defeat. At the age of twenty-four Constantine was supreme in the West.

In the East there had been similar changes, some of which we have noted. Diocletian had abdicated along with Maximian in 305. Galerius became Augustus and appointed Maximin Daia, his nephew, to be Caesar. Together they carried on the persecution of the church. In 307, Galerius made his friend and fellow-soldier Licinius the Augustus to rule Illyria and Macedonia. Licinius was not a persecutor. When Galerius died in 311, Licinius and Maximin Daia shared the rule from Illyria to Arabia. Maximin tried to eliminate Licinius, but Licinius made an alliance with Constantine; he also married Constantine's sister. In 312 they published what is known as the Edict of Milan, which gave the church freedom of worship and returned to her all properties that had been confiscated. Thereupon Licinius went to meet Maximin and defeated him in two battles. Maximin died in 314.

2. The End of Persecution
In the East as in the West, all power was now concentrated

in the hands of one man — Licinius. It soon appeared that two emperors were one too many. Constantine and Licinius fought a battle in 314, but it was not decisive. There was a ten-year peace, during which Licinius turned against Christianity. He thought that an anti-Christian policy would gain him pagan support in the coming struggle with Constantine. In 323, Constantine defeated and captured Licinius, whom he killed a year later. In this war Crispus, the promising son of Constantine, had defeated the fleet of Licinius in a sea-battle. Fausta, Constantine's wife, persuaded her husband that Crispus was trying to kill him so that he could be emperor. Constantine therefore ordered the execution of his son. Later, he discovered that Fausta had lied to him, so he had her killed also. Having thus defeated all his enemies, and having killed his father-in-law Maximian, his brother-in-law Maxentius, his second brother-in-law Licinius, his son Crispus, and his wife Fausta, Constantine reigned alone and unchallenged in the empire. In spite of this unhappy record, we may not take lightly the reports of his conversion. He made Christianity the official religion of the empire; he aided church and clergy with public grants; he sought the peace of the church; he was baptized before he died. Constantine was doubtless fully aware of the record of assassinations from Aurelius to Diocletian. Thus, he probably justified the deaths of Maximian, Maxentius, and Licinius as military necessities. He was certainly patient with Licinius. The dark shadow in his life is the murder of Crispus and the treachery and murder of Fausta. Who shall say with what remorse the mighty ruler of the empire was burdened the rest of his days? Let us turn therefore from this personal tragedy to the joyful words of Eusebius as he describes the end of persecution:

> Men had now lost all fear of their former oppressors; day after day they kept dazzling festival; light was everywhere, and men who once dared not look up greeted each other with smiling faces and shining eyes. They danced and sang in city and country alike, giving honour first of all to God our sovereign Lord, as they had been instructed. . . . Old troubles were forgotten and all irreligion passed into oblivion; good things present were enjoyed, those yet to come eagerly awaited. (*History of the Church,* Bk. 10, par. 9)

QUESTIONS FOR REVIEW

1. Give five examples of the decay of good order in the empire.

2. Mention three major features of Diocletian's reorganization of the empire.

3. What change was made in the position of the emperor?

4. How did the authority of the church in Rome benefit from this reorganization?

5. What were the reasons for the Diocletian persecution? Why did the persecution come as a great surprise to the church?

6. What differences do you see in the first edicts of persecution?

7. What was the difference between the persecution in the West and in the East?

8. What four emperors were involved in the persecution in the East? Do you consider the name "Diocletian persecution" to be accurate?

9. By what military steps did Constantine come to power?

10. How did Constantine bring an end to the persecution?

CHAPTER IX
THE TRINITARIAN CONTROVERSY

In discussing the history of the Apostles' Creed we noted that its primary concern is with the person and work of Christ. The credal witness of the church began with the central declaration that Jesus is the Christ, the Son of God, the Savior of men. This confession was later enlarged with a declaration about God the Father, Creator of heaven and earth, and another about the Holy Spirit and his work.

This centrality of Christ in the faith and witness of the church arises directly out of the New Testament. There he is presented as the Savior of mankind, the head of the church, and as Lord, fully divine and fully human. The early church accepted him as a man, and confessed and worshiped him as God. It placed him on the same level as the Father and the Holy Spirit. It did this naturally and without any feeling of contradiction. The church recognized the mystery of the person of Christ, but rather than debating the mystery it adored and revered it.

This mystery aspect of the person of our Lord has never been lost in genuine Christianity. However, it has often been pressed into the background. This is what happened during the fourth through eighth centuries, when the person of Jesus Christ became a subject of intense theological debate not always very spiritual in character. There were three outstanding reasons for the church's concern with the question:

a. The spread of the gospel to the Gentiles introduced Greeks into the church. The educated Greek mind was highly studious and intellectual. It loved to reflect on difficult problems in theology and philosophy.

b. Greek philosophy made a sharp distinction between the spiritual and the material. Becoming a Christian did not always alter this Greek way of thinking. For the Greeks the creation of the world and the incarnation of the Son of God were major religious and intellectual problems. How can God (pure spirit) create the world (matter) and become man (matter and spirit)?

c. The Old Testament is strongly monotheistic. If Christ is very God, what is his relationship to God the Creator, the God of Israel?

For these reasons it was probably unavoidable that questions about the person of Jesus should arise to which the New Testament gives no direct answer. These questions were of two kinds: the first group concerned the relationship of Jesus Christ to God the Father; the second group of questions dealt with the problem of the relationship between the human nature and the divine nature of Christ. In this chapter we are concerned with the first group of questions.

VARIOUS ANSWERS

The matter is put quite clearly in the first chapter of the Gospel of John:

> In the beginning *was the Word,* and the Word *was with God,* and the Word *was God.* He was in the beginning with God; all things were made through him, and without him was not anything made that was made. . . . And the Word became flesh and dwelt among us, full of grace and truth; we have beheld his glory, glory as of the only Son from the Father. (John bore witness to him, and cried, "This was he of whom I said, 'He who comes after me ranks before me, for he was before me.' ")
> (vss. 1, 2, 14, 15)

In short, how is it to be understood that the Son who in John is called the Logos (i.e., the Word), and who became a human being in Jesus the Messiah, is both *with God* and *is God?* How can God at the same time be one and more than one? How is the Son related to the Father? This was the question before the councils of Nicaea in 325 and Constantinople in 381. The controversy to which this question led laid the basis for the Christian doctrine of the Trinity: it is therefore generally called the Trinitarian Controversy. The church considered various answers to this question before finding a common mind. We shall briefly discuss these answers.

1. The Apostolic Fathers

The Apostolic Fathers wrote between A.D. 90 and 140. Their discussion of the person of Jesus Christ simply repeated the teaching of the New Testament. None of the Apostolic Fathers presented a definite doctrine on this point. In this respect the New Testament, the Apostolic Fathers, and the Apostles' Creed stand in one line.

2. The Apologists

With the Apologists, Greek philosophy became associated with Christianity. The best known of them was Justin Martyr, a man from Samaria whose parents were Roman. He was a student and a teacher of philosophy before his conversion. He remained a philosopher, regarding Christianity as the highest philosophy. He died a martyr for the faith between 163 and 167. Justin taught that before the creation of the world God was alone and that there was no Son. Within God, however, there was Reason, or Mind (Logos). When God desired to create the world, he needed an agent to do this for him. This necessity arose out of the Greek view that God cannot concern himself with matter. Therefore, he begot another divine being to create the world for him. This divine being was called the Logos or the Son of God. He was called Son because he was born; he was called Logos because he was taken from the Reason or Mind of God. However, the Father does not lose anything when he gives independent existence to the Logos. The Logos that is taken out of him to become the Son is like a flame taken from a fire to make a new fire. The new fire does not lessen the older fire.

Justin and the other Apologists therefore taught that the Son is a creature. He is a high creature, a creature powerful enough to create the world but, nevertheless, a creature. In theology this relationship of the Son to the Father is called *subordinationism*. The Son is subordinate, that is, secondary to, dependent upon, and caused by the Father. The Apologists were subordinationists.

3. Irenaeus

Irenaeus, bishop of Lyons in Gaul from 178 to his death in about 203, had the most biblical approach of the early theologians in his discussion of Christ. He was less influenced by Greek thinking and thus more open to a truly biblical view of Christ. He begins his doctrine of Christ with the historical person named Jesus, who was born of the virgin Mary in the reign of Caesar Augustus. Jesus existed before he was born: he was with God before the creation, and all things were made by him. Irenaeus writes:

> If any one, therefore, says to us, "How then was the Son pro-
> duced by the Father?" we reply to him, that no man under-
> stands that production, or generation, or calling, or revelation,
> or by whatever name one may describe His generation, which is
> in fact altogether indescribable. (*Against Heresies,* II, 28:6)

The Son is coeternal with the Father, and it is he who reveals
the Father:

> But there is only one God, the Creator . . . He it is . . . whom
> Christ reveals. . . . He is the Father of our Lord Jesus Christ:
> through His Word, who is His Son, through Him He is revealed.
> . . . But the Son, eternally co-existing with the Father, from
> of old . . . always reveals the Father to Angels, Archangels,
> Powers, Virtues, and all to whom He wills that God should be
> revealed. (II, 30:9)

Beyond this Irenaeus refuses to go. He confesses God the
Creator, God the Son — coexisting and coeternal with the
Father — and he believed that this Son "was very man, and
that He was very God" (IV, 6:7).

The teaching of the Apologists concerning the Son as a
secondary God, and Irenaeus' teaching of the Son as coeternal
with the Father, led many to ask whether Christianity believed
in polytheism. This fear found expression in two very different
conceptions.

4. Adoptionism
One group held the following:

> If the Father is one, and the Son another, but the Father is
> God and Christ is God, then there is not one God but two Gods.
> . . . If God is one, then by consequence Christ must be a man,
> so that rightly the Father may be one God. (Reported by
> Novatian in *Concerning the Trinity,* ch. 30)

Accordingly, in about 195 a certain Theodotus, who came from
Greece to Rome, taught that Jesus was born miraculously of a
virgin (Mary) and that he was a good and righteous man. At the
baptism of Jesus in the Jordan, the Holy Spirit, whom Theodotus called Christ, came upon him. He progressed in goodness, was crucified, and arose again from the dead. Jesus could
be our Savior because of Christ (the Holy Spirit) who was
in him and because his obedience was complete. Therefore,

God adopted him as his Son. The followers of Theodotus were called Adoptionists. The western church did not accept Adoptionism because it could not believe that salvation came by a man, however holy that man may have been. In the East, however, Adoptionism continued for many years. Adoptionism is also called Dynamic Monarchianism, because the one God (*monos* meaning one, plus *arche* meaning rule, i.e., government by one) reveals himself as a divine energy or power (*dunamis*) in Jesus.

5. Sabellianism

A second group held the following, again in the words of Novatian:

> If God is one, and Christ is God, then Christ is the Father, since God is one. If Christ be not the Father, because Christ is God the Son, there appear to be two Gods . . . contrary to the Scriptures. (*Ibid.*)

Like Adoptionism, Sabellianism tried to protect the unity of God. However, it did so in quite a different manner. It taught that God revealed himself in three ways, or modes. He first revealed himself as the Father who created all things and gave the law to Israel. When God undertook the work of salvation, he ceased to reveal himself as Father and took the form or mode of the Son. When the work of the Son was completed, God took the form of the Holy Spirit. Thus the one God revealed himself successively as Father, Son, and Spirit. The Son became incarnate by being born of a virgin, and he died for our sins. According to Tertullian, the Sabellians taught that the Father was born, suffered, and died. They are therefore sometimes called Patripassians (the Father suffers).

Sabellianism was born in Asia Minor and grew up in Rome. It was first taught in Rome about 190 by a certain Praxeas from Asia Minor; he was followed by another Asian, Noetus; and since Sabellius gave the teaching its final form—in Rome about 200—it was named after him. It is also called Modalistic Monarchianism, because the government by one takes place by different modes of revelation of the one God. Sabellianism had longer life than Adoptionism, but it survived in the East rather than in the West.

6. Tertullian

The most influential answer given in the West was proposed by Tertullian. Indeed, it provided the foundation for the answer that the Catholic Church was to give to the problem at Nicaea in 325 and again at Constantinople in 381. Tertullian taught that there is one divine *nature*. The Father and the Son have this one nature in common. They are separate and distinct, however, so far as their *persons* are concerned. Therefore, there is one divine nature, but there are two divine persons. Each of these has a specific function. At the same time, Tertullian gave a distinctly subordinate place to the Son. The Son is not eternal. The eternal God *became* Father when he begot the Son, just as he *became* Creator when he made the world. On this point Tertullian is one with the Apologists. Later theology united Tertullian's teaching of one nature and two persons with Origen's teaching of the eternal generation of the Son (see Chapter VII) to give the Catholic answer to the question of the relationship of the Son to the Father. Finally, Tertullian also related the Holy Spirit to the Father and the Son. Three divine persons exist in one divine nature. Thus Tertullian provided the main outlines for the Christian doctrine of the Trinity.

7. *Arianism*

Up to this point the Trinitarian debate had taken place entirely in the West. We now move to the East, where the debate became a great controversy. It lasted sixty years, involved the entire eastern church, the western church in part, and occupied the attention of eleven emperors.

The long discussion began with Arius, a presbyter in the church in Alexandria. He was a disciple of Lucian, who in turn was a student of Paul of Samosata, bishop of Antioch from 260 to 272. Paul was an Adoptionist (Dynamic Monarchian). He taught that the Logos or Reason of God dwelt in the man Jesus. This Logos had also been in Moses and in the prophets; in Jesus, however, it was present in much larger measure. As a result, he was united with God in a relationship of love as no other man had been. Therefore, God "adopted" Jesus after his crucifixion and resurrection and gave him a sort of deity. Three synods in Antioch dealt with Paul's teaching, and the third one (in 269) condemned and excommunicated Paul.

These views deeply influenced Arius. Like the western Adoptionists, he was concerned about the unity of God. Therefore, he taught that the Father alone is without a beginning. The Son (or Logos) had a beginning; God created the Logos in order that he might create the world. Since the Logos was the first and highest of all created beings, Arius was willing to call the Logos God. But this was only a manner of speaking. The Logos was a creature. And God himself could not create the material world; indeed, Arius considered God so far removed from men that it was impossible to know him or to have fellowship with him. Arius was thoroughly Greek in his conception of God.

Arius' view of Christ was much inferior to that of either Theodotus in the West or of Paul of Samosata in the East. In their view, the man Jesus whom God adopted was fully and truly human. Not so the Jesus of Arius. In his teaching, Jesus had a human body but not a human soul. The Logos took the place of the human soul in Jesus. He was therefore a creature who was neither God nor man. He was not God because the Logos that was in him was created; he was not man because he did not have a soul. Moreover, the Logos was subject to change: he could become a sinner.

Such was the teaching which Arius began to set forth in about 311. Alexander, the Catholic bishop of Alexandria, convened synods which condemned his views, and he was forced to leave Alexandria. Nevertheless, he gained a great following. There were three reasons for this:

a. His views seemed to protect the unity of God against the danger of polytheism.

b. They satisfied the deep-rooted Greek idea that God cannot be the creator of the material universe.

c. They gave high honor to the Son or Logos of God and even declared him to be God.

The controversy spread to all parts of the East. Theologians, monks, and church leaders took sides in the debate. The common people did not understand the issues, but nevertheless they aligned themselves with this or that view.

THE COUNCIL OF NICAEA

No one followed the situation more closely than Constantine. His political eye saw that the unity of the empire was in danger. Politically, the empire was one; theologically, it was two. Therefore he determined to call a council of the entire church. It would settle the issue, and he would enforce its decision with the power of the state. In calling the council, Constantine was not primarily concerned with establishing a true view of Christ's relationship to the Father. His aim was to maintain a united empire. It was the task of the council to formulate a Christology that would serve this end. Thus, it was a combination of controversy in the church and the resulting political uncertainty in the empire that brought the first ecumenical council into being. It was held in Nicaea in Asia Minor and met in 325 from May 20 to July 25. Three hundred bishops attended, of whom all but a few were from the East. The Roman bishop sent two delegates. Hosius, the aged bishop of Cordova in Spain, was Constantine's chief ecclesiastical adviser.

It soon became clear that there were three parties at the council. A small group supported the full position of Arius; it was led by Eusebius, bishop of Nicomedia. Another small group supported Alexander, bishop of Alexandria. Between these two parties stood a large middle group led by Eusebius of Caesarea, reportedly the most learned man of his time. It held to a Christology which rejected Arianism but with which Alexander and his followers could not agree. Eusebius of Caesarea believed in one Lord, Jesus Christ,

> the Logos of God, God of God, light of light, life of life, the only-begotten Son, the first-born of all creation, begotten of the Father before all ages. . . .

Alexander felt that this statement left room for the Arian view. He wanted a statement that could possibly be read in an Arian way. In this he was supported by Hosius and the emperor. The council therefore expressed belief in

> one Lord, Jesus Christ . . . very God of very God, begotten not made, consubstantial *(homoousios)* with the Father, by whom all things were made. (Nicene Creed)

The council also rejected those who teach that "there was when he was not," or "before his generation he was not," or that the Son of God was created, or changeable, or of another substance than the Father. Any who believed these errors was anathematized (i.e., declared accursed).

Arius and five other delegates refused to sign the creed of Nicaea. Eusebius of Nicomedia refused to sign the anathema. All these were exiled. Peace did not follow these decisions and actions. Few seemed to know what *homoousios* really meant. Debate continued. Ecclesiastical and imperial politics became so confused that it was not possible to tell where the one began and the other ended. This situation was to continue for nearly sixty years. The central word around which the whole debate turned was the term *homoousios* (from the Greek *homo,* meaning same, plus *ousia,* meaning nature, substance, or being). Is the Son of the *same* nature as the Father, or is he not? That was the great issue.

FROM NICAEA TO CONSTANTINOPLE

In the midst of this controversy, and continuing nearly to its end, stood one of the greatest figures of the early church. He was Athanasius, the successor of Alexander as bishop of Alexandria. He was born in Alexandria about 300 and died there in 373. He helped to formulate the decision of Nicaea, and he spent the remainder of his life defending it. A man of strong and noble character, he had great ability as a leader and administrator. He was the leading theologian in the church. He was sympathetic to monasticism, and the Egyptian monks were among his strongest supporters. As theologian and church leader, he overshadowed all others between Origen, who died in 253, and Augustine, who was born in 354.

1. The Theology of Athanasius

His theology and faith were controlled by the thought expressed in II Peter 1:4: ". . . that . . . you may escape from the corruption that is in the world because of passion, and become partakers of the divine nature." Here we meet perhaps the chief difference between the theology of the West and the theology of the East. In western theology the central problem is the removal of the guilt of sin. We have offended God, we stand guilty before him, and we cannot again enjoy his favor unless our sin is removed. This is done by Christ through his incarnation, life, death, and resurrection.

In the East the central problem was not human guilt but human corruption. Man as the head of creation has lost God's image and has become spiritually and morally depraved. In order to save his creation God became man. In Christ the human nature is united to the divine nature, and in him man's corrupt mortality is changed into a beautiful immortality. Through faith in him we become partakers of the divine nature. "He was made man," said Athanasius, "that we might be made divine." Without a fully divine Christ who is also fully human there cannot be salvation. Arius did not believe in either the one or the other. Therefore, Athanasius opposed him with all the strength of his mind and heart.

After Nicaea it became apparent that only the West and the party of Athanasius were satisfied with the *homoousios* of Nicaea. The party of Arius felt completely defeated. The large middle party of Eusebius of Caesarea felt that it should not have agreed with *homoousios*. Sabellian theologians had used that word to describe how the Son was related to the Father. Eusebius and his followers hence feared that the door had been left open for the Sabellian heresy. Soon the parties of Arius and Eusebius united to remove the *homoousios* from the creed. They gained the support of Constantine. He dismissed Hosius as his theological adviser and appointed Eusebius of Nicomedia, the leader of the Arian party at the council. In 335 a synod in Antioch declared Athanasius deposed and Constantine sent him into exile in Gaul.

2. *Politics and Theology*

In 337, Constantine died and his three sons inherited the empire. Constantine II received the far western part: Britain, Gaul, and Spain. Constantius received the far eastern part: Macedonia, Greece, Thrace, Asia Minor, Palestine, Syria, and Egypt. Constans received the area lying in between: Italy, North Africa, and Illyricum. Both Constantine II and Constans took the western position and supported Athanasius. Constantius supported the Arians. In 340, Constantine II was killed in battle with the forces of Constans, leaving the empire divided between Constans in the West and Constantius in the East. In 350, Constans was assassinated by the rebel German emperor Magnentius. Three years later Constantius defeated and killed the latter. Thus, by 353 the entire empire was in the hands of an emperor sympathetic to the Arian position. Having the full power of the empire, Constantius decided that the religious question should now be decided once and for all. In councils held in the West at Arles and Milan, he forced the western bishops to abandon Athanasius, and he exiled some of their leaders. In 357 a council held in Sirmium in Illyria forbade the use of *ousia* (nature) in speaking of the relationship between the Father and the Son. With this the *homoousios* of Nicaea became a dead confession. This was a complete victory for the Arians. They could now deny any real relationship between the Father and the Son and still be within the creed of the church.

The large middle party, which had so far worked together with the Arians, became frightened by this new development. They were by no means ready to deny a very real relationship between the Father and the Son. They were not ready to say that this relationship was a *sameness* of nature; however, they did believe that there was a *similarity* in the natures of the Father and the Son. A new word entered the debate, namely *homoiousios* (from *homoi,* meaning like, and *ousia,* meaning nature). The middle party and the Athanasian or Nicene party now began to enter into conversation with each other. They discovered that the "like" nature of the middle party was not very different from the "same" nature of the Athanasian party.

FINAL STAGES

1. Julian

Meanwhile, a significant political development took place. In 361, Constantius died and was succeeded by his cousin Julian. When Constantine the Great had died in 337, every relative who might have claimed the throne was killed except his three sons. Julian's father was among those who were massacred. Julian was allowed to live because he was only six years old. He was brought up by Constantius and received an education in strict accord with eastern orthodoxy. No one knew that he hated Christianity because of the murder of his father and brothers, or that he had secretly studied pagan philosophy and religion. When he became emperor he sought to turn the empire back to paganism. For that reason he has been called Julian the Apostate. History records that he was a just and capable emperor. He died in 363 in battle with the Persians. As part of his religious policy in the empire, he required that the persecution of the supporters of Nicaea be stopped. He recalled Athanasius from his third exile, but sent him away again in the same year when many pagans were converted to Christianity through him. Nevertheless, effective persecution of the Nicene party had come to an end.

2. The Three Cappadocians

Athanasius died in 373. His last years were peaceful. He

did not live to see full official victory for the Nicene cause, but there were two major reasons for him to believe that it would triumph. One we have already noted: the *homoousios* and the *homoiousios* parties were discovering that their views were very much alike. The second reason was that three younger and influential theologians were making full agreement more and more likely. They were Basil of Caesarea (in Cappadocia), Gregory of Nazianzus, and Gregory of Nyssa. Since all were from Cappadocia, they came to be known as the Three Great Cappadocians. They represented a post-Nicene orthodoxy.

For Athanasius the unity of God had been a certainty and the divine Trinity had been a mystery. His problem had been: how can the one God exist in three persons? The three Cappadocians asked the question the other way around. For them the certainty was the Father, the Son, and the Holy Spirit, and the mystery was: how can Father, Son, and Holy Spirit be the one God? Athanasius began with the one God and tried to understand how the three persons were related to him. The Cappadocians began with the three Persons and tried to understand how the one God was related to them. The end result of seventy years of study, discussion, controversy, and political strife was the acceptance of Athanasius' one God in three persons and of the Cappadocians' three persons in one God. These were the two sides of the one confession of the Triune God.

Whether one regards the God of Scripture from the one side or the other, or from both together, mystery will always be an inseparable element in the divine being. Perhaps no one has been more helpful on this subject than Augustine. He compared the Trinity to love, the highest human virtue, in the illustration that the Father is the lover, the Son the loved one, and the Spirit the love that unites them. But Augustine could not penetrate to the center of the mystery either. When he was asked, therefore, why he had written so large a work as *The Trinity* to discuss this mystery, he said, "I speak in order not to be silent."

3. The End of the Controversy

A final paragraph must conclude this summary of the great controversy of the fourth century. In 379, Theodosius became emperor in the East. He was born in Spain in 346, the son of a distinguished general in the Roman armies of the West. As a

Christian in the western church, Theodosius stood committed to the Nicene theology. This he enforced when he became emperor. In 381 he convened the Council of Constantinople, which confirmed the faith of Nicaea and threatened with exile all who professed the Arian faith. With this action Arianism came to an end in the empire, surviving only among the Germanic tribes. Among them it died out in the seventh century.

QUESTIONS FOR REVIEW

1. Why did the person of Christ become a matter for serious study and debate in the first centuries of the church's history? Which early theologian had the soundest view of the problem? Why?

2. What were the differences between the Adoptionist, the Sabellian, and the Arian points of view?

3. Why did Arianism become the most influential heresy concerning Christ?

4. What did the Council of Nicaea mean when it said that the Son is *homoousios* with the Father?

5. Why did Athanasius make the declaration of the Son's *homoousios* the foundation of his whole life and ministry?

6. How did imperial politics influence the course of the debate from Constantine's death to the death of Athanasius?

7. How did the theology of Athanasius and that of the three Cappadocian Fathers come together to close the debate?

CHAPTER X

THE GERMANS, ARIAN MISSIONS, AND MONASTICISM

This chapter is chiefly concerned with those peoples and tribes outside the Roman Empire who lived east of the Rhine and north of the Danube rivers. Collectively they are often referred to in historical literature as the "barbarians." It is therefore useful to know what the word "barbarian" means. The Greeks called all foreigners *barbaroi*: it meant people who were strange, foreign, or crude, especially in speech. The Romans adopted this word. From the time of Augustus they called all people who were neither Greeks nor Romans *barbari*. It implied the idea of inferiority to Graeco-Roman civilization. However, many of the barbarians were, in fact, very intelligent. The Germans in particular had standards of morality and duty that the Roman historian Tacitus, for example, envied. They observed the high cultural, economic, and agricultural development of the empire and desired it for themselves.

THE RHINE AND THE DANUBE

It is important at this point to remember the great significance of the Rhine and Danube rivers in the history of the Roman Empire. From the time of Augustus — that is, for three hundred and fifty years — these two great rivers had formed the northern boundaries of the empire. All the land area east of the Rhine and north of the Danube was the land of the *barbari*. Along this line Rome had stationed no less than fourteen legions of its highly trained soldiers. These, together with their supporting troops (called auxiliaries), would number almost 200,000 men. Thus, from the North Sea to the Black Sea a river barrier defended by the best-trained army in the world kept the Germans out of the Roman lands.

As the empire grew weaker and weaker, the threat of invasion became increasingly greater. Between 370 and 500, the Germans broke through the river defenses and poured into the empire. In the course of the fifth century the invaders completely overran the empire in the West. In 476 a German chieftain named Odovacer deposed the western emperor, a boy of eleven years. With that event, the western empire ceased to exist. The Germans established states of their own. They adopted Roman civilization insofar as they were able. Europe, and to a large extent even Italy, the home of Roman civilization, became predominantly German. Many countries and provinces of countries in Europe today are named after German tribes: France after *Franks;* England after *Angles;* Denmark after *Danes;* Sweden after *Suines;* Lombardy (in Italy) after *Lombards:* Burgundy (in France) from *Burgundians;* Saxony (in Germany) and Essex and Wessex (in England) from *Saxons;* Friesland (in Holland) from *Frisians.*

THE GERMAN MIGRATIONS

The history of the Teutons, or Germans, as they are more commonly called, is very much like that of the Bantu in central Africa. The latter's original home was in Zaire (formerly the Congo). From this base they first spread to the east and to the west, then northward and southward. These migrations occurred over hundreds of years. Stronger tribes drove out weaker ones; distinct languages and customs developed. Separate states with their own laws and areas of influence came into being. Interestingly, the word "Bantu" (from *ba ntu*) means people, which is also what the word "Teuton" (from *teuth*) means.

Between the years 2000 and 1000 B.C. the tribes called the Germans lived in lower Scandinavia, in Denmark, and just south of Denmark, between the Elbe and the Oder rivers. This period of time corresponds roughly to Israel's history from the time of Abraham to King David. They had no civilization in the usual sense of the word. They lived in the forests by hunting and in more open areas by herding; they did not take up farming until hunting and herding areas became limited. They had no written language. Thus, the early Germans were far behind the civilizations of Egypt, Babylon, and Assyria, with which they were contemporary.

About 1000 B.C., the Germans who lived in Denmark and south of Denmark began to move westward. They stopped at the Rhine and moved south along its eastern bank. Some continued westward to the North Sea. Four centuries later, another great German migration began to take place farther to the north. Between the years 600 and 300 B.C., German tribes living in the lower Scandinavian peninsula (southern Norway and Sweden) began to move south. They crossed the Baltic Sea to the area lying between the Oder and Vistula rivers. They continued to move southward between these rivers, and a number of them crossed the Vistula to the east. Some of the Germans found a place to settle in central Europe. Others, particularly the large tribe known as the Goths, moved in a southeasterly direction and settled in the general area of the Black Sea.

While these migrations were going on, Rome was growing and expanding. First it conquered Italy, North Africa, and Spain. Thereupon it moved eastward, up to the Persian border. Finally, it conquered Gaul to the north and Egypt and the Mediterranean coast to the west of Egypt. By A.D. 150 the empire was at its greatest extent. By 350—the point at which we have arrived in this history—Romans and Germans were facing each other across the Rhine-Danube frontier. The Romans were weakening, and the Germans were becoming more and more numerous and were pressing to enter the land of plenty across the rivers.

THE VISIGOTHS

With this general picture of the Germanic migrations before us, we shall from now on be chiefly concerned with one German tribe, the Visigoths (which means West Goths, in distinction from the Ostrogoths, or East Goths). They had been permitted to live in the Roman province of Dacia, north of the point at which the Danube enters the Black Sea.

1. Huns, Goths, and Romans

About A.D. 350 a people known as the Huns emigrated from central Asia into southeastern Europe. Their fighting men were fierce and merciless warriors whom no people could resist. They totally defeated the Ostrogoths between the Dniester and the Dnieper rivers, as well as the Visigoths, who had gone to help their brothers. With no defense between them and the advancing Huns, the Visigoths begged the Roman emperor to permit them to cross the Danube into the empire proper. The emperor did not have sufficient forces to meet the Huns himself, and there was no time for calm reflection on the matter. He therefore allowed the Visigoths to cross the river with the understanding that they would surrender their weapons. On their arrival in the empire, problems of food and land caused unhappy differences between them and the Romans. Roman officials treated them scornfully, and some Visigoths were even sold into slavery. After two years, German pride was so offended and Roman patience so exhausted that war was unavoidable. In 378 the two armies met, and the Visigoths utterly defeated the Romans. The emperor Valens was killed. The defeat of the Romans in the battle of Adrianople is one of the decisive events in the history of the Western world. It was the beginning of the end of the Roman Empire as it had existed up to that time, and it made possible the rise of nation states in Europe.

2. The Wanderings of the Visigoths

The Visigoths decided not to remain in the area south of the Danube, which the Romans had given them. They began to wander in the empire, and their journey was marvelous indeed. First they tried to take Constantinople. Failing in this, they moved after some years into Greece. From there they moved slowly northward along the coast of the Adriatic Sea. After several attempts, they entered Italy and sacked Rome in 410. Continuing southward in Italy, they tried to cross into the fertile lands of North Africa. However, a storm destroyed the ships in which they were to sail. They moved back to the north of Italy and crossed the Alps into Gaul. They continued westward and crossed the Pyrenees into Spain, where they set up a kingdom that lasted for nearly three hundred years. They also set up a kingdom in central and southern France. For a time it looked as though Europe had a mainly Visigothic future. But this was not to be.

In their efforts to prevent the Visigoths from entering Italy, the Romans had called back most of their armies from the Rhine frontier. This left Gaul open to the German tribes east of the Rhine. In 406 these tribes streamed across the river and settled in Gaul, Spain, and as far as Africa. The most powerful tribe that invaded Gaul was the Franks. They lived where the Rhine enters the North Sea, and they had also been permitted to live in the empire. With the Roman defenses now gone, they conquered Gaul area by area and were master of it by 500. By that time smaller kingdoms had arisen in Italy, Spain, North Africa, along the North Sea from the Rhine to Denmark, and in Britain. In this way the western Roman Empire came to an end, and the foundations were laid for the nation states of western Europe.

With this we conclude our brief account of German origins, migrations, and settlements. It is among the descendants of these peoples that the church in Europe developed. It is they who became the main carriers of Christianity throughout Britain, Gaul, Scandinavia, and all of Europe east of the Rhine and north of the Danube. This fact is all the more remarkable because when the Germans entered the empire most of them were Arians. Their conversion to the faith of Nicaea is one of the turning points in the history of the Christian church. We will now turn to that story.

ARIAN MISSIONS

When the persecutions ended, Christians formed about ten percent of the population of the empire. It is understandable that so small a minority, often persecuted, did not think of missions beyond the Rhine and the Danube. Indeed, when the gospel began to spread among the Germans, it was not the church in the empire that took the first step. It was a Goth. His name was Ulfilas (little wolf) and he was an Arian. It was largely the result of his work that the Goths, and through them the German tribes generally, came to accept Arian Christianity.

1. Ulfilas

The earliest introduction of Christianity among the Goths took place between A.D. 250 and 300. It arose out of the witness of Christian prisoners taken in Visigoth raids in Asia Minor. However, there was neither Christian leadership nor organization nor systematic instruction until Ulfilas began his work. He was born about 310 in the Goth country north of the Danube. His mother was a Greek Christian who had probably been taken prisoner in a raid. Ulfilas learned the Christian faith from her, but his upbringing was Gothic. He therefore knew the Gothic people, their language, and their customs. He gave leadership to the small group of Christians in the area in which he lived. He learned to speak Greek from his mother, and through her he was kept aware of the church and the empire from which she had come.

In 341 he was among a party of Goths who had been sent to Constantinople, perhaps as a diplomatic delegation. While in the capital city, he came to the attention of Eusebius, bishop of Constantinople. Eusebius ordained him bishop of the Gothic Christians. Since Arianism was strong in the eastern part of the empire at that time, it was natural that Ulfilas be Arian in his belief. For seven years he served his people beyond the Danube. A serious persecution against them under a Visigoth chieftain led Ulfilas to ask for permission to settle in the empire south of the Danube with them. This permission was given. Ulfilas accompanied the Christians and served them until his death in 383.

2. The Gothic Bible and the Spread of Christianity

The greatest service of Ulfilas was the translation of the Bible into Gothic. Since the Goths had no suitable writing, he invented an alphabet using mainly Greek letters. The Gothic Bible was very influential in the conversion of the Goths. (Ulfilas did not translate I and II Kings because he feared that reading about Israel's wars would make the Goths more warlike than they already were.) From the Visigoths the gospel spread to the Ostrogoths and other German peoples. We do not know the identities of the men and women who spread the gospel among them, what means were used, what routes were followed, or what resistance the preaching met. We do know that when the Germans began to enter the empire in great numbers, most of them were Arian Christians at least in name.

This circumstance had two very important results. One is that the invasion of the empire by the Germans was far less destructive than is often thought. Having adopted the religion of the empire, they were also eager to receive its civilization. Romans and Germans lived alongside each other more as neighbors than as enemies. The second result was closely related to the first. The difference between the Catholic Christianity of the Romans and the Arian Christianity of the Germans created religious and social problems. Each form of Christianity had its own church organization and its own forms of worship. The religious difference helped to strengthen social differences, so that fellowship and intermarriage were difficult. These differences, however, were gradually removed by an event that occurred in 496.

3. *Clovis and the Franks*

The Franks were one of the few German tribes that did not become Arian. They had remained pagan, probably because they were at the opposite end of Europe from the Visigoths, from whom Christianity had begun to spread. In the end, it appeared that they were the most powerful of all the Germans: between 450 and 500 they conquered most of Gaul. Their king, Clovis, realized that sooner or later his people would have to choose between Arian and Catholic Christianity. He saw how numerous the Catholic Christians were in Gaul (which had been part of the empire since 50 B.C.), how strong the church was, and how influential her bishops were. He may well have believed that he would govern more successfully if he were on the side of the church rather than against it. He may also have declined to put his faith in a savior who was neither God nor man. At any rate, he married a princess from a German tribe that had accepted Nicaean Christianity. He allowed their first child to be baptized in the Catholic Church. In 496 he and many followers were baptized as Catholic Christians. The conversion of Clovis led to the conversion of the Franks as a people. Some years later, the Burgundians, a large German tribe that lived in Gaul, became Christian. One after another the German tribes followed the example set by Clovis and the Franks. By 650 all had turned to the Catholic faith, and Arianism died out, never to be revived again.

THE RISE OF MONASTICISM

We noted that the Germans who invaded the empire desired Roman civilization and its benefits. However, this does not mean that they knew how to manage and use that civilization when they got control of it. Many were unable to read or write; they had never constructed the kinds of roads, bridges, and buildings that were common in the empire; they had never administered a stable, complex government or made laws for a developed community. The Germans were therefore quite incapable of maintaining the civilization which had come into their possession. They did not try to destroy it, but all its beauty decayed and disintegrated in their hands. They were like a farmer who obtains a tractor he does not know how to use. It soon becomes a piece of rusted metal.

1. The Church and Civilization

In the midst of this collapse there was one institution that did not collapse: the church. The church had an organization; therefore, there could be communication between places distant from each other. The church had a history; therefore, its past provided lessons for the present and directions for the future. It preached a message that was the same everywhere; therefore, men could have a common religion, a common hope, and a common moral law by which to live. In the midst of confusion the church provided stability and order; amid all the hatreds it worked for reconciliation; in all the sorrow it offered comfort.

In rendering these services the church did far more than perform purely spiritual duties. It fed the hungry, released prisoners, resisted corruption, preserved books and made new ones; it taught farming, carpentry, and animal husbandry, and it conducted schools. In a time when many had lost all things, the church became all things to all men. It was a strong center around which a world that had lost its direction could gather and find a new purpose for living. The church prepared men for the life that is to come and preserved civilization for the life that now is.

The chief means in the hands of the church for performing these great services were the monasteries. We shall conclude this chapter by considering the early history of monasticism in the western church.

2. The Ascetic Way of Life

There have always been men and women who value the ascetic way of life. In the area of religion, an ascetic is one who denies himself bodily needs in order to set his mind on spiritual matters. The continual practice or mode of life in which this is done is called asceticism. The word "ascetic" comes from the Greek word *askein,* which means to exercise or to train. It was used of athletes preparing themselves for contests. The religious ascetic may therefore be said to be a spiritual athlete.

When the church became free from persecution, it also became worldly. Many who had no real interest in salvation entered the church. Worship became formalized and lost much of its power. Thousands of Christians who glorified martyrdom no longer had any martyrdom to endure. Moreover, the Greek belief that the body was the cause of sin influenced much Christian thinking. For these reasons many Christians embarked on an ascetic way of life in order to remain close to God and not become lost in concerns of this life.

One such man, an Egyptian named Anthony, went to live by himself in the desert. This simple act was the beginning of the large and tremendously important movement known as monasticism. Anthony was born about A.D. 250. When he was twenty years old, he began to practice asceticism after he had heard the text read in a church service, "If you would be perfect, go, sell what you possess and give to the poor . . . and come, follow me" (Matt. 19:21). At first he lived an ascetic life in his town. This probably included abstinence from certain kinds of food and drink, from social and recreational enjoyments, from marriage, and from ordinary comforts of life; particularly, it included the observance of set times of prayer and other religious exercises. This, however, did not fully satisfy him. After fifteen years he went into the desert to live completely alone so that there would be nothing to take his attention away from religious devotion. He lived this severely ascetic life for twenty years. He gained the respect and devotion of ascetic followers who came to live near him. They asked him to teach them how the ascetic life should be lived. At last he yielded to their entreaties and instructed them by word and example until his death in 347. When the religiously ascetic life is lived in a collective and organized way, it is called monasticism.

3. Two Kinds of Monasticism

The ascetics whom Anthony taught followed his way of life, which was to live alone in constant meditation, prayer, and worship. It is true that they lived close together. However, each one lived in a hut alone, meditated, prayed, and worshiped alone, and secured and prepared his own food. Sometimes two or several might live together. As the movement spread, hundreds and even thousands lived in the same area. This was the Antonian form of monasticism.

Soon another form of monasticism developed. It was not individual but communal in character. Its founder was also an Egyptian, a young man named Pachomius, who was born about 290 and had served as a soldier in one of Constantine's armies.

On returning home, he became an ascetic of the Antonian type and went to live with a hermit monk along the Nile. Recognizing the shortcomings of this kind of asceticism, he organized a communal kind of monastery. Its members came to number several hundreds. Their entire day was regulated: it provided opportunity for religious exercises, physical work, eating, and sleeping. All lived under a common rule, ate from a common kitchen, and united in daily worship. Work was considered necessary not only to live but to be human.

Thus monasticism gave order and system to the ascetic way of life. The Antonian form stressed the ascetic life lived *alone;* the Pachomian form stressed the ascetic life lived *in community.* Both forms soon spread beyond Egypt. Palestine adopted chiefly the Antonian kind, Greece the Pachomian type. Italy and Gaul first tried the individual form but later adopted the communal kind of monasticism. We must here take note of the role that Athanasius played in the spread of monasticism. It will be recalled that Athanasius was bishop of Alexandria from 328 to 373. He was therefore a countryman and a contemporary of both Anthony and Pachomius. Athanasius was ascetically inclined himself; he admired and encouraged the monastic life. He visited the monks in their desert areas, and both Anthony and Pachomius were his friends. In fact, Athanasius wrote a biography of Anthony. When Constantine sent him into exile in Gaul, he spread in that country his enthusiasm for monasticism. In his second exile from 339 to 346 he did the same in Italy. It spread to Spain and North Africa. Great church leaders like Augustine, Ambrose, and Jerome supported it.

MONASTICISM IN EUROPE

In Europe, however, the Antonian type of monasticism had serious disadvantages. It was distinctly Egyptian in character. This meant that it was practiced in generally warm weather, whereas in Europe it is cold much of the year. It had also been deeply influenced by Indian asceticism. In this form individualism, self-inflicted suffering, and long meditation were common. European character was less inclined in these directions. What Europe needed was a monasticism that provided greater protection against cold and wet weather, and was more communal and less severe in character. Benedict of Nursia brought such a monasticism into being.

1. Benedictine Monasticism

Benedict was born about 480 in the town of Nursia, near the city of Spoleto in central Italy. He came from a good family and attended school in Rome. The immorality he witnessed in that city led him to become a monk in the Antonian mode, and he lived this life for three years. Seeing that solitary monasticism had disadvantages, he organized a communal monastery as Pachomius had done in Egypt. Benedict soon had so many disciples that he had to organize twelve monasteries to receive them. His work as a reformer of monastic life took place in the monastery at Monte Cassino, which he established in 520. He died about 550.

In the light of his experience as a monk, first in a solitary, then in a communal situation, Benedict wrote a rule to govern the life of his monks at Monte Cassino. This life was so well-suited to European conditions that in time it spread to Gaul and to England, and from there was carried to the areas east of the Rhine. Some of the main provisions of Benedict's Rule were:

1. Each monastery was governed by an abbot. He was elected for life and his word was final in all matters.

2. Both abbot and monks lived under the law of the Rule. The abbot, for instance, was bound to consult with all the monks in important matters and with senior monks in lesser matters before making final decisions.

3. There were definite hours for religious exercises, for work, for eating and sleeping.

4. Monks were bound to the monastery for life, and were therefore not free to move from monastery to monastery. They formed a family, therefore, which lasted for life.

5. Life in the monastery was regular and disciplined, but it was not subject to physical suffering, as had been the case among the Egyptian monks.

6. Each monastery remained completely separate and independent from all other monasteries.

7. The central purpose of the monastic life was to grow in the love of God. The means to this end were the reading of Scripture, prayer and song, and the exercise of obedience and humility. Benedict's Rule called the monks

in honour to prefer one another. Let them bear most patiently with each other's infirmities, whether of body or of character. Let them contend with one another in their obedience. Let no one follow what he thinks most profitable to himself, but rather what is best for another. Let them show brotherly charity with chaste love. Let them fear God and love their abbot with sincere and humble affection, and set nothing whatever before Christ, who can bring us to eternal life.

Benedictine practice spread among women as well as among men. Nunneries following Benedict's Rule appeared in Europe and increased in number. They were especially prominent in England. They were influential not only religiously but also socially and educationally. In England the nunneries' inhabitants were mainly women of the wealthier segments of society.

2. Irish Monasticism

A distinctive and influential type of monasticism developed in Ireland. It was introduced by Patrick, an English Christian who was also the founder of Irish Christianity. It was Egyptian in form, a mixture of Antonian severity and Pachomian communal life. It developed in the fifth century and was intensely mission-minded and civilizing in character. Between 500 and 800, Irish monks evangelized Ireland, Scotland, and northern England. They also went as missionaries to Europe. The most educated men during this period were trained in Irish monasteries.

3. Benefits of Monasticism

The reason for discussing monasticism in the context of the German peoples can now be seen. When the Germans entered the empire in large numbers in the fifth century and later, Roman life and society did not immediately break down. The process of decay took place step by step over many years. By the year 600, it had advanced very far. By that time, however, both Benedictine and Irish monasticism had begun to spread in western Europe and the British Isles. For the next six hundred years, education and other civilizing influences were almost entirely in the hands of the monasteries. With few exceptions, only the clergy were educated. Even Charlemagne, the greatest king of the Middle Ages, gained most of his knowledge not through reading but through readers. Monks became not only church leaders but philosophers, architects, the chief advisers of kings, expert farmers, musicians, glass-makers, builders, and masters of many other skills. The larger monasteries copied the great books of the past and kept them safely in their libraries. Many monks spent their lives in this work. Therefore, it is not too much to say that the monasteries were the chief agents in evangelizing Europe, in preventing the loss of many early Roman and Christian literary works, and in making the Germans part of both the church and the civilization it protected.

QUESTIONS FOR REVIEW

1. Describe again the relationship of the Rhine and Danube rivers to the empire.

2. When did the Germans break through the river boundaries? How do countries and areas in Europe today reflect ancient Germanic occupation of the land?

3. What is similar in the population spread of the Bantu in central Africa and that of the Germans (or Teutons) in Europe?

4. How are Germans, Goths, Ostrogoths, and Visigoths related? Indicate the travels of the Visigoths. Can you give approximate dates for certain points in their long journey?

5. How did Christianity begin among the Germans? What kind of Christianity did they accept? Explain.

6. What effect did the conversion of the Germans have on their invasion of the empire? What special role did the Franks play in the religious history of the Germans and of the church in western Europe?

7. How was monasticism related to the Germanic invasions and the collapse of the empire?

8. Where did Christian monasticism originate? What were the causes of its rise? What two main kinds were there?

9. How did the Benedictine form of monasticism differ from that of Anthony and Pachomius? How was this related to cultural and climatic circumstances?

10. What services did monasticism render in Europe to the church and its people?

CHAPTER XI

THE LIFE OF THE CHURCH, 312-600

After Constantine became emperor, the life and organization of the church began to differ greatly from its life and organization in the earlier years. The church had ceased to be regarded as an enemy of the state and was now in alliance with it. Membership in the church had once been dangerous; now it became advantageous. The poet, the philosopher, the artist, the politician, the military officer, the architect and the banker worshiped openly with the laborer, the farmer, and the trader. The church had become an accepted and important part of the richest and most powerful empire in the ancient world.

The new circumstances in which the church found itself deeply influenced every part of its existence. It remained the people of God, but this people lived, thought, worshiped, and was governed very differently from the Christians who had passed through the shadow and fire of persecution. The areas in which these changes appeared most prominently were:

1. The government of the church.
2. Its relationship to the state.
3. The way in which the church worshiped.

In discussing the new situation, we shall repeatedly refer to the history of the church before Constantine became emperor in 311. We shall refer to this history as the first period of ancient church history, and the history from 312 to 600 as the second period.

THE GOVERNMENT OF THE CHURCH

The close association between the church and the Roman Empire may seem like the association of a mouse with an elephant. This did not long remain so. The ecclesiastical mouse never became an imperial elephant, it is true, but it became large enough and influential enough to compel the elephant to reckon with it. When emperors stooped to kiss the ring on the bishop's finger, and when bishops were courageous enough to rebuke the emperor and even to forbid him the sacrament, we see something larger than a mouse-elephant relationship.

1. Differences Between the Two Periods

At no time in the first period did the church have an empire-wide structure of government. All authority was local in character. The monarchical bishops in the larger cities had significant influence within the areas which they governed. They began to hold local synods in the second century. There was fellowship and contact of various kinds between the different parts of the church. Generous hospitality was given to Christian travelers, and their membership in distant churches was recognized. However, there was no common government, no common church law, no common church action.

In the second period this changed radically. Three years after Constantine became emperor in the West, he called a synod to meet in Arles, Gaul, to represent the whole of the West. Its purpose was mainly to deal with the Donatist troubles in North Africa. Eleven years later, the same emperor called the first ecumenical council in Nicaea. From then on, holding of councils became common in the life of the church. They were held as far apart as Gaul and Syria. Their decisions were binding in the areas in which they were held. Sometimes they had church-wide significance. They became important factors in creating common belief, unity, and order in the church.

During the second period the church also strengthened and expanded the form of government that had begun to develop in the first period. It will be recalled that the most prominent and influential church authorities in the second and third centuries were the monarchical bishops. They governed the areas of their authority with the help of presbyters and deacons. During the second period this simple form of government became more complicated.

At this time the distinction between the laity and the clergy became prominent. The laity were the mass of the Christian community who had no office. The clergy were church officials who were set apart from the laity by ordination. As time went on, the whole — or nearly the whole — of the church's work fell into the hands of the clergy. Since this work was constantly increasing, it became necessary to create new offices to perform it. As a result, the clergy developed into three large groups: the lower clergy, the higher clergy, and the episcopate.

2. Orders of Clergy

The lower clergy consisted of exorcists and readers, who had minor roles in the services of the worship, and acolytes and sub-deacons, who formed the secretarial staff of the bishop.

The higher clergy were the deacons and presbyters. The care of the poor, originally entrusted to the deacons, was now discharged by the lower clergy. Deacons became the chief administrative assistants of the bishops. For example, Athanasius was a deacon when he served Bishop Alexander as secretary at the council of Nicaea. Presbyters conducted services and administered the sacraments; they were thus the spiritual arm of the bishop. Later they were called priests. The higher clergy arose out of the lower: at thirty they were eligible to become deacons; at thirty-five deacons could become presbyters; at forty-five a presbyter, so far as age was concerned, was eligible to become a bishop.

The episcopate consisted of the bishops of the church. The lowest in rank was the country bishop. Next in order was the city bishop. Both the country bishop and the city bishop were subject to the archbishop, called metropolitan in the East, who was the bishop of the capital city of a province. The archbishops in turn were under the authority of the patriarchal bishops.

3. The Patriarchal Bishop

At the beginning of the fourth century there were three patriarchal bishops in the Catholic Church. They were the bishops of Rome, Antioch, and Alexandria. When Constantinople became the capital of the empire under Constantine, the bishop of that city became a patriarch. At the council of Chalcedon in 451, the bishop of Jerusalem was similarly honored, although he never became influential. In the fifth century the Patriarch of Constantinople governed the church in twenty-eight Roman provinces, the Patriarch of Antioch in fifteen, of Jerusalem in four, of Alexandria in nine, and of Rome in the whole of the West, representing sixty-seven provinces. The Patriarch of Rome has from the beginning been called the Pope, and he is called that today.

The structure of church government here described is called hierarchical. When the word is used religiously, hierarchy is an ecclesiastical form of government. Like a pyramid, the structure moves from lower clergy at the base, through higher clergy and different grades of bishops, to the single authority at the top. The term hierarchy comes from the Greek word meaning rule by priests.

CHURCH AND STATE

During the first period of ancient church history, that is, up to Constantine, the church dealt with all its problems ecclesiastically. That is to say, all matters of doctrine, discipline, worship, and government were settled *by the church*. The state had no representation or voice in the affairs of the church. With Constantine this situation changed completely. The emperors before Constantine had seen the importance of religion for the unity of the empire, and Constantine saw this as clearly as they. Therefore, he followed exactly the same policy that his predecessors had followed — with one difference. For the earlier emperors, Roman religion was the unifying factor that they encouraged; for Constantine it was Christianity. The pagan emperors built pagan temples; Constantine built churches. The pagan emperors supported the Roman priests; Constantine gave grants to the Christian clergy. The pagan emperors suppressed Christianity; Constantine and the Christian emperors who followed him gradually but surely suppressed paganism and heresy. At first paganism was *religio licita* and Christianity was *religio illicita*. At the end of the fourth century, Catholic Christianity was *religio licita,* and Arianism and paganism had become *religio illicita.* Everything had changed. Yet, in a sense, nothing had changed.

1. The Donatist Controversy

The deep and far-reaching relationship between church and state which Constantine introduced began almost from the time of his victory over Maxentius in October 312. A few months later the church asked him to settle what is known as the Donatist controversy. It had developed in the following manner. In 311 a new bishop named Caecilian had been ordained in Carthage. One of the bishops who participated in the ordination was Felix of Aptunga, who was accused of surrendering the scriptures in the recent persecution. Therefore, the accusers of Felix considered the ordination of Caecilian invalid. The church officially supported Caecilian, but many bishops opposed him. The North African church was split in two. The opponents of Caecilian elected their own bishop named Marjorinus. Each side excommunicated the other. Both sides appealed to Constantine in 313 to settle the dispute; he accepted their appeal and called a synod to meet in Rome. It declared Felix to be innocent of the charges made against him and decided in favor of the election of Caecilian. The matter was complicated by the fact that Constantine had given financial assistance to the church in Carthage (the Caecilian party) but not to the new church of Marjorinus. The church split remained, indeed became worse. In 314, Constantine called a much larger assembly to meet in the city of Arles in Gaul. It was the first council to meet in the West, and it also supported Caecilian. The schism in North Africa only increased in extent and bitterness. In 316, Constantine intervened forcibly. He took away the churches of the protesters and exiled all their bishops. Among these was Donatus, who had succeeded Marjorinus and who gave the separatist movement its name. Constantine's action did not bring peace. In 321 he gave up efforts to enforce his decree. He was as helpless against the Donatists as earlier emperors had been against the Christians. At that time, however, it had been pagans persecuting Christians; now it was Christians persecuting Christians. The Donatist schism remained strong for about one hundred years. After that, it gradually died out as a result of Augustine's teaching concerning the church and suppression by the government.

2. The New Church-State Relationship

Thus began the relationship between the Christian church and the secular state. The handling of the Donatist controversy established a pattern for dealing with any religious issue that threatened the unity of the empire: a) the emperor would call a synod or council when that seemed to be necessary; b) he would allow the synod or council to settle the issue; c) if the decision was not acceptable to any party involved, the emperor would enforce the decision by the power of the state. This pattern was followed in the convening of the Council of Nicaea and in many subsequent instances.

It was by no means in the holding of councils alone that church and state worked together. This cooperation came to expression in many other ways. Of this the following are examples:

a. The clergy was excused from taxation and from public services, which were often burdensome. This favor led many wealthy men to enter the ministry so that they would be excused from paying taxes. This in turn led the government to forbid rich men to become ministers.

b. The church received grants of money from the state and was allowed to receive legacies. As a result of this, the church became independently wealthy in lands, houses, and other properties. In the Middle Ages it came to own as much as forty percent of all the land in Christian Europe.

c. Bishops had the right to settle disputes between Christians in their own courts, and these ecclesiastical courts and their decisions were enforced by the law of the empire.

d. Bishops were allowed to intercede for prisoners, criminals, and others accused in the secular courts. They could even intercede with emperors on behalf of cities and provinces with which the emperor was displeased.

e. Various kinds of work and amusement were forbidden on Sunday, as well as the collecting of taxes and private debts.

f. The church influenced the state to enact more humane legislation to protect widows and orphans, prisoners, poor, and slaves.

g. The influence of the church contributed to the liberation of women from their traditional bondage, and secured the end of gladiatorial shows.

3. Disadvantages of the Relationship

It is clear that, on the one hand, the church was enabled to render many services which it had not been able to perform before. But it is also clear that the church was exposed to many temptations that did not exist before its alliance with the state. State politics entered the church, and the church entered into the politics of the state. Discipline became lax and church membership was for many a wholly outward matter. The needs of the church were no longer met primarily by the sacrifices of its own members, but were received from the state and from the church's own properties and investments. Clergy became influential in the larger and smaller communities and received even higher honors than officials of the state received. In the first period, a true picture of the church was reflected in Paul's words in the first chapter of I Corinthians: "For consider your call, brethren; not many of you were wise according to worldly standards, not many were powerful, not many were of noble birth; but God chose what is foolish in the world to shame the wise. God chose what is weak in the world to shame the strong, God chose what is low and despised in the world, even things that are not, to bring to nothing things that are, so that no human being might boast in the presence of God'' (vss. 26-29). During the second period, in many areas it was no longer possible to describe the church in this way.

The policies and the association between church and state begun by Constantine were continued by his sons Constantine II, Constans, and Constantius. Julian the Apostate reigned less than two years, dying in battle with the Persians in June 363. His reputed dying words, ''Thou hast conquered, O Galilean,'' are probably legendary, but they express an historic fact. With Julian every effort to restore paganism to its earlier place of influence and prestige in the empire came to an end.

4. Continuation of the Relationship

The successors of Julian continued the close church-state relationship. During the reign of Theodosius (378-395) it reached a climax. In 381 he convened the second ecumenical council in Constantinople. This council accepted Nicaean Christianity as the faith of the empire and brought to an end the seventy-year-old dispute between the Catholic and the Arian views of the relationship of the Son to the Father. Theodosius thereupon forbade the practice of Arianism as well as pagan religion in the empire. With this as a precedent, the persecution of heresy by the state became common. It was practiced throughout the Middle Ages and was considered a proper policy by both Roman Catholics and Protestants during and after the Reformation.

Thus it may be said that Constantine and his successors set the pattern for church-state relationships that endured for more than thirteen hundred years. Even today remnants of the early relationship can be found. Vatican City, in which church and state are one, is the abiding Roman Catholic witness to its belief in the close relationship between the church and the state. On the Protestant side, the clearest instances are found in Scandinavian countries: Denmark, Norway, Sweden, and — closely related — Finland. The relationship between church and state in Sweden is representative:

> The Swedish Constitution provides for a general Assembly of the Church to be convened by the King and to consider business which he presents. Decisions of the General Assembly are not

final but are presented as petitions for the approval of the King and Parliament. On the other hand, the General Assembly can veto religious bills that have passed the Parliament. In fundamental matters the state is not to impose its will contrary to the will of the Church, nor is the Church to make significant changes that are not considered and approved by the nation through the political system of the whole community. (M. Searle Bates, *Religious Liberty*, International Missionary Council [1945], p. 108)

THE WORSHIP OF THE CHURCH

The change in the life of the church after Constantine became emperor found notable expression in its worship. During the time of trouble the emphasis in the church's religious life had been on things inward and spiritual. For more than two centuries it did not have the skills or the wealth or the opportunity to erect costly buildings and arrange for elaborate ceremony in them. In the forty years prior to the Diocletian persecution, Christians had built spacious churches in many cities. They had thought that with the persecutions under Decius and Valerian (251-259) their afflictions had come to an end. But these churches were all destroyed. Eusebius the historian writes: "I saw with my own eyes the places of worship thrown down, from top to bottom, to the very foundations" (*The History of the Church*, Bk. 8, Sec. 2).

Constantine and his devout mother, Helena, led the way in erecting new and more costly structures. Before the year 400, there were forty large churches in the city of Rome alone. Within the churches, religious ceremony became more complicated in form. The architects, musicians, artists, designers of furniture, vestments, and metalware, the composers of hymns and liturgies — all these now found means to express their faith not only spiritually but outwardly, with appeal to eye, ear, and imagination. The "church in the house" of New Testament days had become the church of the basilica and the cathedral.

This expression of religious ideas and feelings in art, architecture, and music was not always understood and appreciated. The masses who entered the church were often pleased with the ceremony and beauty without understanding their meaning. Moreover, the worship that developed was often man-made and without warrant in Scripture. The multiplication of holy days, the veneration of saints, martyrs, and relics, and the value attached to pilgrimages and holy places often pushed truly spiritual concerns into the background.

In the two preceding sections we noted the development in the government of the church and in church-state relations during the fourth, fifth, and sixth centuries. We shall conclude this chapter with a brief review of the way in which the church worshiped during this period.

1. The Church Year

Man has been so created that he lives his life in certain regular patterns that are constantly repeated. These patterns may be called cycles. There are the cycles of day and night; work and rest; birth, growth, decline, and death; there is the cycle of wet season and dry season in the tropics, and spring, summer, fall, and winter in colder regions. The two (or four) seasons make a year. For convenience this natural year has been divided into months, weeks, and days, called the calendar year.

As there is a natural year, so the Christian world recognizes a spiritual year. This year is generally called the church year, and its beginnings go back to the very early history of the church. The church year developed around the celebration of three great redemptive acts of God: the Incarnation (Christmas), Christ's death and resurrection (Easter), and the coming of the Holy Spirit (Pentecost).

The Christmas celebration was preceded by four weeks of Advent. During these weeks, especially on Sunday, the worship centered on the coming of Christ. Christmas was a day of rejoicing and the giving of gifts, with services commemorating the birth of our Lord. The celebration of Easter was preceded by six weeks of Lent (meaning Spring). These weeks fixed the attention on the suffering of Christ; thus they were a time of fasting. Lent climaxed in Good Friday and was followed by the joy of the Easter celebration. Pentecost means fifty days, representing the seven weeks lying between the resurrection and the coming of the Holy Spirit. On the fortieth day, the church celebrated the return of Christ to the Father in the feast of the Ascension. These were joyous weeks as the church continued to remember the Easter event and looked forward to the celebration of the Spirit's coming. Pentecost was the last of the three great festival cycles. The remaining Sundays until the next Advent, varying from twenty-two to twenty-seven, were devoted to regular worship and the building up of the church's life in the power of the Pentecostal Spirit.

2. Sunday and Sunday Worship

From the beginning, Christians had remembered and celebrated the first day of the week as the day of Christ's resurrection. Under Constantine it received legal as well as religious meaning. In 321 he decreed:

> On the venerable Day of the Sun let the magistrates and people residing in cities rest, and let all workshops be closed. In the country, however, persons engaged in agriculture may freely and lawfully continue their pursuits; because it often happens that another day is not so suitable for grain-sowing or for vine-planting; lest by neglecting the proper moment for such operations the bounty of heaven should be lost.

It is noteworthy that Constantine did not relate his legislation to Christian practice or to the Fourth Commandment. He designated Sunday by its traditional pagan name, the Day of the Sun, not the Sabbath or the Day of the Lord. Pagans could therefore accept it. Christians gave the natural sun a new meaning by thinking of Christ the Sun of Righteousness. Both Constantine and later emperors, as well as church councils, enacted additional Sunday legislation. It was Constantine's decree of 321, however, that laid the basis for the universal recognition of Sunday as a day of rest.

In the Christian community public worship was the chief activity on Sunday. The worship service consisted of two parts: that which was meant for all, including catechumens, and that which was meant only for the communicants. At the conclusion of the first part, all but the communicants were dismissed. This dismissal (from the Latin *missus*), which signaled that the communion service was about to begin, gave its name to the service of communion — the *missa,* from which the English word mass is derived.

In the public service, selections were read from the Gospels and the Epistles. Sometimes selections were read from the Prophets. The Psalms were sung. Since there were very few Bibles, private reading of Scripture during the week required going to the church to read; not many did this. To this was added the unhealthy teaching that the Bible was intended to be read only by the clergy. Since the clergy in the West presumably knew Latin and those in the East knew Greek, there was no translation of the Bible into the vernacular languages, with the exception of the Gothic Bible.

The sermon, preached in the first part of the service, occupied an important place in the worship of the eastern church. In the western church preaching was often poorly done, and the communion service stood in the foreground. Preaching was a less solemn exercise in the early church than it is today. When the preacher made a strong point, or even if he spoke beautifully or acted dramatically, the audience often applauded. Both Chrysostom in the East and Augustine in the West protested against the practice, but they were not heeded.

Participation in communion could be daily, on each Sunday, or less frequently. In the eastern church, communion (or the Eucharist) became such a mysterious affair that it was deemed proper to celebrate it only once a year and on very special occasions. The western church encouraged more frequent participation. Some councils required attendance at communion at least three times a year: at Christmas, Easter, and Pentecost. In the fifth or sixth century, communion became a public service, although it remained open only to those who had been confirmed.

3. The Sacraments

The validity of baptism and the Lord's Supper as proper sacraments was never questioned in the early church. However, the validity of other sacraments was in question for a long time. Confirmation and ordination were being practiced as sacraments in the fifth century. Ambrose, bishop of Milan, held that foot-washing was a sacrament. Matrimony, penance, and extreme unction were added later. The present seven sacraments of the Roman Catholic Church were not fully established until the twelfth century. In addition to baptism and the Lord's Supper (the Mass), it holds to the sacraments of confirmation, ordination, penance, extreme unction, and matrimony.

The Reformation recognized only baptism and the Lord's Supper, regarding the others as ecclesiastical or religious usages that do not have the status of sacraments. The mode of baptism in the New Testament is immersion and appears to have been administered only to adults. The unity of the covenant in the Old and New Testaments, and the teaching that there is no salvation outside the church, eventually led to the practice of infant baptism: Origen (185-254) speaks of it as common, and in the fifth century it was the general practice of the church. We cannot here discuss the much debated question of the Lord's physical presence in the sacrament of communion. However, it is clear that, like so many fundamental theological and ecclesiastical questions, its origins lie in the thought and practice of the early church.

4. The Saints

It was natural for the early Christians to hold the apostles in loving memory, especially Peter and Paul, as well as Stephen, the first martyr, Mary, the mother of Jesus, John the Baptist, and the great prophets of the Old Testament. It was not long, however, before the church added to these the names of martyrs who had suffered in the persecutions and others known for their spiritual life. Such were ascetics like Anthony, bishops like Athanasius and Ambrose, and godly women like Monica, the mother of Augustine. Christians began to pray to them as their intercessors with Christ. In the New Testament, all believers are called saints; in later church history, only great people such as martyrs or church leaders were saints, and that only after they were dead. Nowhere in the Bible are we directed to pray to them or told that they can help us. Nevertheless, the lists of saints became longer and longer, and the great leaders of the church supported their veneration.

In the fourth century, Mary, the mother of Jesus, began to stand out as the greatest of all saints. Called "the mother of the Lord" in the New Testament, she became known in the fifth century as the "mother of God." A virgin before the birth of Jesus, she was now known as a virgin from her mother's womb to her death. It was declared that she was sinless from her birth and after her death became "the Queen of heaven," more prayed to than Christ himself. The Arian controversy had so stressed the deity of Christ that his humanity had become vague and almost unreal. Mary now virtually took his place as a very warm and gentle human and heavenly being to whom men might turn in their need.

In this way a hierarchy of local, national, and universally

acknowledged saints, each with his or her special power, came to stand between the believer and God. The Son of God, as the only Mediator between God and men, was eclipsed by a host of higher and lower saints to whom prayer could be made. Moreover, they had power not only in heaven with God but also on earth with man. This aspect of saint worship we must note as the final subject of this chapter.

5. Holy Days, Holy Relics, and Holy Places

The saints were of varying fame and influence. There were local saints, national saints, and saints that were honored everywhere in the church. There were saints for cities and countries, for trades and professions, for travelers and even for sicknesses. Each saint received a day on which to be remembered. The great saints were remembered with great festivals on their days. Soon two or more saints had to be remembered on the same day because there were not enough days in the year for each saint to have one.

There is perhaps no point at which paganism influenced Christianity more clearly and openly than in the veneration of saints. The belief that the holy dead can help the living was accompanied by the belief that things which belonged to these saints could help the later owners of such things. Bones, fingernails, bits of hair, clothes, books, and other articles that belonged to the saints came to be venerated and adored. Such relics were placed under the altar and thus were thought to lend increased holiness to the worship. Many of these relics were found years — even centuries — after the death of the saint. The mother of Constantine was said to have discovered the very cross on which Christ was crucified. To this very day, the stairway which Christ ascended into the court of Pilate is said to be in Rome and is visited yearly by thousands of pilgrims. Before long, a vigorous trade in relics developed. Despite Helena's claim that she had discovered the true cross, innumerable splinters from the cross were found throughout the church.

The common custom of making pilgrimages to holy places is in the same spirit of the veneration of relics. Of course it is interesting and useful to see where the great figures of Christian history lived and are buried. It helps to illustrate more clearly to our minds their services and their persons. This was not, however, the primary purpose of pilgrimages in the early church. Christians in the early church believed that making pilgrimages had religious merit, that they contributed to obtaining salvation, and that they gave a certain holiness to the pilgrims who made them. This idea of pilgrimage was basic to the crusades held in the eleventh, twelfth, and thirteenth centuries. In that effort, whole armies from Germany, Italy, France, and England sought to reconquer the Holy Land from the Muslims in order to bring its holy places under Christian control again.

QUESTIONS FOR REVIEW

1. How did the government of the church in the second period of ancient church history (311-600) differ from that of the first period (up to 311)?

2. What was the difference between lower clergy, higher clergy, and episcopate? What was a patriarchal bishop? How many were there in the empire? Where?

3. Mention five ways in which church and state cooperated.

4. What is your opinion of the relationship between church and state that came into being under Constantine?

5. How did the new church-state relationship affect worship?

6. What is meant by "the church year"? How does the church year come to expression in your church?

7. How did saints, holy days, places, and relics come to play a role in the life of the church? Do any of these play a role in your denomination?

CHAPTER XII

FOUR GREAT CHURCH LEADERS

The church, like any true community, consists of both people and leaders. The two belong together: the people produce leaders, and the leaders in turn influence and guide the church. We have seen something of the example and work of leading figures like Ignatius, Polycarp, Justin Martyr, Irenaeus, Tertullian, Origen, Athanasius, Benedict of Nursia, and others. What would have become of the church without their leadership? But also, how would they have come to the faith and to their task without the church? In the study of church history it is important, therefore, to take note of the lives of great men in the church as well as the church's life as a whole.

At this point we shall review the lives of four men who greatly influenced the church in the second period of its early history: Ambrose, bishop of Milan; Chrysostom, patriarch of Constantinople; Jerome, translator of the Latin Bible; and Augustine, bishop of Hippo and one of the most influential figures in the long history of the church. All were contemporaries: Ambrose, Chrysostom, and Jerome were born between 340 and 345; Augustine was born in 354. Ambrose and Augustine belonged to the western church, Chrysostom to the eastern. Jerome spent the larger part of his life in the West, but he did much of his work in the East and died there. They not only richly served the church of their own time, but their example and work continue to inspire and serve the church of later generations.

AMBROSE (340-397)

Ambrose was born in Treves (Trier), the capital city of Gaul. His father was the governor of all of Gaul, Britain, and Spain and was therefore one of the most powerful men in the empire. When Ambrose was thirteen years old, his father died. He continued his education in Rome and studied to become a lawyer. He so distinguished himself in his chosen profession that at the early age of thirty he was appointed governor of Upper Italy. There, in the large capital city of Milan, he governed with justice and gentleness and became respected and loved by all.

1. Election as Bishop

In 374 the bishop of Milan died. Since there was rivalry between Arians and Catholics in the election of a new bishop, Ambrose went to maintain order in the church where the election was being held. In the midst of the proceedings, a child's voice cried out, "Ambrose bishop!" The whole gathering — Catholic and Arian alike — took up the cry. Ambrose was elected bishop, and the assembled bishops approved the choice. He was only thirty-four years old, and since he had not yet been baptized, he protested his election. The protests of Ambrose were ignored just as the rules of the church governing the election of bishops had been ignored. Ambrose then accepted the action of the people and the bishops as a call from God that he could not reject, and he gave himself to his new and unexpected task.

Being wealthy, he gave away all his riches and property to the poor and the church. His office was always open to the poor and the oppressed. Any time that he could spare from his daily duties as bishop he gave to the study of the Bible and theology. He preached often — sometimes daily — and it was through hearing him preach that Augustine turned to the Christian faith. Ambrose refused to attend banquets or to use the riches of the church for himself. He lived as an ascetic to the end of his life.

2. Character of his Administration

Ambrose was a convinced Catholic and resisted the Arians wherever he could. The emperor Valentinian II was a fourteen-year-old boy whose mother, Justina, governed for him. She was Arian in her sympathies and demanded equal rights for Arians to worship in Milan. Ambrose refused and Justina yielded. He also secured the election of Catholic bishops and the deposition of Arian bishops outside his own diocese. It is understandable that the Arians regretted that they had helped to elect him bishop.

Ambrose was not always fair to his opponents. In Mesopotamia, Christians had destroyed a meeting place of Valentinian Gnostics and had burned down a Jewish synagogue. The emperor Theodosius ordered the local Christian bishop to rebuild both at the church's expense. This so angered Ambrose that he not only protested to the emperor in writing but in a sermon publicly appealed to him to cancel the order. So great was Ambrose's influence that the emperor withdrew his instruction.

The greatest moment in the life of Ambrose, and doubtless one of the greatest moments in the history of the entire church, came in a far more serious confrontation between him and Theodosius. The emperor was a Christian, but he was also a rough and hot-tempered soldier. In 390 the people of Thessalonica in Macedonia caused a riot and murdered an army officer. So great was Theodosius' rage that he sent an order for the mass slaughter of townspeople. After dispatching the order, he regretted his action and sent another order to cancel it. But it was too late. Before the cancellation arrived, the army invited the people to a spectacle in the stadium. When the stadium was full, the soldiers locked the gates and slaughtered all inside. Some seven thousand people were killed that day.

On hearing this, Ambrose wrote a firm pastoral letter to Theodosius, rebuking him and calling on him to repent. Theodosius, who had now made Milan his capital, did not heed the appeal of his bishop. On a Sunday shortly thereafter he went to attend worship at the cathedral. Ambrose, dressed in his full bishop's robes, met him in the porch of the church, openly rebuked him, refused him entrance, and told him to depart and repent. For some months Theodosius did not attend divine services. "The Church of God," he complained, "is open to slaves and beggars. To me it is closed, and with it the gates of heaven." Ambrose remained firm. Then the emperor, being a Christian at heart, confessed his sin and implored the forgiveness of God and man, lying stretched out full length on the floor before the whole congregation.

Ambrose, more than any other leader in the early church, proclaimed in word and deed the independence of the church from the state. He has left for all time an imperishable example of fearlessness and courage in speaking the law and the gospel to the great and powerful in the earth. Yet he was gentle in heart, and he stooped as a true shepherd of Christ to help the poor and the oppressed in their need.

JEROME (345-420)

Jerome (sometimes referred to by his Latin name, Hierony-
mus) occupies a quite distinct place in the history of the church.
He is not, like Ambrose, remembered for his loving character
and administrative ability; nor, like Augustine, for his warm
piety and theological greatness. Jerome was a linguistic scholar, and he was a notable ascetic. He gave to the western church
a remarkably reliable translation of the Bible, and by example
and writing he greatly furthered the cause of monasticism. Although he made other contributions to the life of the church,
it is chiefly for these two that he is remembered.

1. His Asceticism

Jerome was born in the province of Pannonia, which lies
north of Illyricum. He was reared in a Christian home. At
the age of eighteen he went to Rome to continue his schooling
and, like Ambrose, became a lawyer. After traveling about in
Gaul and practicing the ascetic life for three years in his home
area, he went to Antioch to visit the eastern church. Meanwhile, his heart was pulled in three directions. As a student
he loved the great Latin writers, especially the orator Cicero.
As a Christian he felt he should give his life to the study
of Scripture. As an ascetic he felt drawn to the monastic life.
What was he to do?

While in Antioch, he resolved to go into the desert and
live the life of a hermit. This he did for five years, seeking
to kill the temptations of the mind by suffering in the flesh.
His description of his sufferings illustrates the inability of any
man to escape from himself:

> How often, when I was living in the desert, in the vast soli-
> tude which gives to hermits a savage dwelling place, parched
> by a burning sun, how often did I fancy myself among the
> pleasures of Rome! I used to sit alone because I was filled
> with bitterness. . . . My face was pale and my frame chilled
> with fasting; yet my mind was burning with desire, and the
> fires of lust kept bubbling up before me when my flesh was
> as good as dead. . . . I remember how I often cried aloud
> all night till the break of day and ceased not from beating my
> breast till tranquility returned at the chiding of the Lord.
> (Letter xxii, par. 7)

It was during these years in the desert that Jerome had the dream that changed the course of his life. In the midst of a fast which was so severe that he thought he would die, he was suddenly

> caught up in the spirit and dragged before the judgement seat of the Judge; and here the light was so bright, and those who stood around were so radiant, that I cast myself upon the ground and did not dare to look up. Asked who and what I was, I replied, "I am a Christian." But he who presided said: "Thou liest, thou art a follower of Cicero and not of Christ, for, 'where thy treasure is, there will thy heart be also.' " Instantly I became dumb, and amid the strokes of the lash — for he had ordered me to be scourged . . . I began to cry and to bewail myself, saying, "Have mercy upon me, O Lord, have mercy upon me. . . ." I made oath and called upon his name, saying: "Lord, if ever again I possess worldly books, or if ever again I read such, I have denied thee." Dismissed then, on taking this oath, I returned to the upper world . . . thenceforth I read the books of God with a greater zeal than I had previously given to the books of men. (Letter xxii)

2. The Latin Bible

The desert years also made him familiar with the Arian controversy, which was at that time nearing its end. He wrote to Pope Damasus in Rome asking him for advice with respect to it. Thus began a fruitful relationship between Jerome and the Pope which was to lead him to his life work. In 382, while attending a synod in Rome with his bishop, he became the theological adviser of Pope Damasus. It was in the course of this association that Damasus interested Jerome in revising the Latin Bible. To understand the great importance of this work we must know something about the then existing versions of the Bible.

In 250 B.C. Jewish scholars had translated the Old Testament into Greek, the translation known as the Septuagint. This was a great gain. However, there was also a great loss. Increasingly, the Greek Christian world lost contact with the Hebrew Old Testament. The loss was made greater by the fact that so few Jews became Christians. Moreover, the Septuagint was not in all respects an accurate translation. Mistakes in the translation were multiplied by faulty copying, by making copies from copies, and — perhaps most of all — by the translation of the Septuagint into Latin. In fact, various Latin translations were made and, as before, copies were made from copies. Jerome saw that a satisfactory Latin translation could be made in only one way: the Old Testament had to be translated directly from the Hebrew.

Meanwhile, Jerome strongly encouraged the ascetic life in Rome. His most devoted followers were women from wealthy families. These he taught both Scripture and the manner of the ascetic life. When Pope Damasus died in 384, Jerome decided to go to Palestine to do his translation work. Some of his most promising pupils in Rome went with him. Among them were the wealthy Paula and her daughter Eustochium. They settled near Bethlehem, where they built a monastery, a convent for women, a church, and a hostel for pilgrims from all parts of the church. Here Jerome lived the remaining thirty-four years of his life, until his death in 420. He had learned Hebrew and Chaldee while a hermit in the desert. Now, surrounded by books, copyists, and Jewish language assistants, he studied and translated, working at his great task of translation, as well as writing many other books.

In 405, after twenty years of work, Jerome finished the translation of the Latin Bible. It is called the Vulgate (from the Latin *vulgata versio,* meaning common version). It is the official Bible of the Roman Catholic Church to this day. It was indeed providential that so thorough and reliable a translation was prepared for the western church before the knowledge of Greek and Hebrew almost completely disappeared in the West.

3. *Writings and Character*

Jerome also wrote a number of commentaries on books in both testaments. He wrote books on church history and doctrine. Many letters have been preserved from his vast correspondence with friends and leaders throughout the church. Again and again he entered into debate with or criticism of leading figures in the church, writing treatises against them. Of all this writing the commentaries and the letters were most useful. The commentaries greatly helped the church in the understanding of Scripture. The letters provide us with a remarkable description both of Jerome's inner life and of the times in which he lived.

Jerome is acknowledged as one of the saints of the church.

The title of saint has been given to members of the church, both men and women, who were noted for their pious character, holiness of life, and miraculous powers. The qualities of piety and holiness in Jerome were often obscured by weaknesses of character. He was proud, jealous about his place in the church, often unfair in criticism, and capable of abusive language in writing. The title "saint" is therefore more one of honor because of his great services than of merit because of his godliness.

JOHN CHRYSOSTOM (347-406)

In Chrysostom we meet one of the greatest preachers in the history of the church, a man of great courage, which was not, however, always accompanied by great wisdom. As a result, his name is great in the church, his reward is great in heaven, but on earth it was death in exile.

1. Ascetic Habits

John (who only long after his death was called Chrysostom, meaning golden mouth) was born in Antioch of Syria about 347. His father was a highly placed general in the eastern Roman army. He died while John was a child, leaving his wife Anthusa a widow at the age of twenty. Because she was a devout Christian, she did not remarry, according to the Christian custom of the time. She dedicated her life to the care of her son and daughter. Her influence on John was enduring.

John studied under Libanius, the famous teacher of literature and oratory in the East. He was a pagan who rejoiced when Julian tried to restore paganism in the empire, and wept when he died. John was so brilliant a student that when Libanius was asked who should replace him at his retirement, he replied, "John, but the Christians have stolen him from us." John's career, like that of Augustine, was interrupted by baptism in 370. He put away all thought of earthly success as a lawyer and decided to become a monk. His mother prevented this, at least for a time. She begged him not to become a monk until after her death. He heeded his mother's plea, lived at home with her, but followed a monastic life, eating only enough to remain healthy, sleeping on the floor, and spending much of his time in meditation and prayer.

In 374, Anthusa died and Chrysostom went to live as a

monk in a mountainous district south of Antioch. There he fasted, studied, meditated, prayed continually, and wrote the first of his books. He pursued the monastic life so severely that in 380 he had to return to Antioch for reasons of health. The bishop of Antioch ordained him as a deacon, and in this work he came to know the people in their daily needs, especially the poor. A few years later he became a presbyter. This permitted him to preach, and Chrysostom began the work for which he is chiefly known, that of a great and effective popular preacher.

2. The Preaching Patriarch

Antioch was one of the notable cities of the Roman Empire. Its history dated from 300 B.C. It was not only a political but also a great commercial center: the trade from Asia Minor, upper Euphrates, Egypt, and Palestine met there. It was in Antioch that believers in Christ were first called Christians, and from there Paul carried the gospel to the Gentiles. After the fall of Jerusalem, Antioch was for many years one of the leading centers of Christianity. At the time of Chrysostom, nearly half of its more than 200,000 inhabitants were Christian. Constantine had given Antioch its largest and most beautiful church, and it was there that Chrysostom preached. For fourteen years he addressed vast crowds, exhorting them to simple faith and uprightness of life. During these years he also wrote with high praise concerning the monastic life, virginity, and continued widowhood after the death of the husband.

So great was Chrysostom's popularity and influence that when Nectarius, the patriarch of Constantinople, died, he was elected to that high office. The immorality against which Chrysostom had preached in Antioch was even greater in Constantinople. Moreover, there was the plotting and the gossip surrounding church and state politics in the imperial capital. Theophilus, the patriarch of Alexandria, was jealous of Chrysostom's influence and wanted to overthrow him, even though it was he who had ordained him. Eudoxia, the wife of the emperor Arcadius, was a pleasure-loving woman who disliked Chrysostom's strong moral sermons. She led a plot against him, and he unwisely preached about Elijah's rebuke to Jezebel. False charges were made against Chrysostom, and he was sent into exile. But before he could be taken out of the country the people demanded his return and threatened a revolt. At that time an earthquake shook Constantinople, and it was said to be felt most severely in Eudoxia's bedroom. The empress repented in terror, and Chrysostom was brought back in triumph.

3. Exile and Death

Soon, however, the battle broke out again. The empress caused a silver statue of herself to be erected in the public square in front of St. Sophia, the great cathedral in which Chrysostom preached. The noise of the dedication of the statue disturbed the worship service and led to Chrysostom's renewed criticism of the empress. It is reported that he used words such as these: "Again Herodias is raging, again she is dancing, again she demands the head of John on a platter." Since in those days Chrysostom was known only as John, the empress considered the parallel of herself to Herodias and John (Chrysostom) to John the Baptist complete. Again Theophilus and Eudoxia joined forces, and Chrysostom was banished a second time, this time permanently. He was arrested in the cathedral during a baptism and exiled to Armenia. Exercising continued and even greater influence in exile than in Constantinople, he was driven still further into a lonely wilderness. He died while traveling to his last place of exile, praising God and forgiving all who had treated him unjustly.

Perhaps the best-known prayer in Christendom, after the Lord's Prayer, is the petition written by Chrysostom, which is a regular part of the Anglican liturgy and frequently prayed in other churches:

> Almighty God, who has given us grace at this time with one accord to make our common supplications to thee; and dost promise that when two or three are gathered together in thy name, thou wilt grant their requests: fulfil now, O Lord, the desires and petitions of thy servants, as may be most expedient for them, granting us in this world knowledge of thy truth, and in the world to come life everlasting, Amen.

AUGUSTINE (354-430)

Augustine was the ancient church's most distinguished son. He was great in heart and great in mind. Because he was great in heart, he was great in faith, love, and humility. Because of this he was for centuries the most influential theologian of the church. We shall conclude this biographical chapter with a sketch of his life and some indication of his writings and influence.

1. Early Life

Aurelius Augustinus, known in history as Augustine, was born in Tagaste, a small town in North Africa near the city of Hippo. His father was at first a pagan but received baptism before his death in 371. Monica, Augustine's mother, was one of the most godly women in Christian history. Her constant love and spiritual concern for her son was probably the deepest religious influence in Augustine's life. Although he was a catechumen, Augustine did not become a Christian until later. Like many in his time he lived with a young woman but did not marry her. They had a son whom they named Adeodatus (meaning given by God). Augustine studied in Carthage to be a lawyer, and when he had finished his studies he went to Rome with his concubine and their son to seek employment as a teacher. In all his studying and religious seeking he found no satisfying faith or philosophy to guide him. At the same time, he could not forget the prayers and admonitions of his mother. His search for a position as a teacher took him to Milan, where he came under the influence of Ambrose, who was then approaching the height of his influence in that city. Augustine went to hear him more because of his eloquence as a speaker than because of his preaching of the gospel. Gradually, however, Ambrose's powerful sermons began to make an impression on him. Furthermore, his mother came to live with him, and persuaded him to send his concubine away and to become engaged to a girl who was not yet old enough to marry. Feeling that he should lead a pure life, but being unable to do so, he exclaimed to God, "Give me chastity, but not yet." And he took another concubine.

2. Conversion and Ordination

It was in this situation that Augustine entered upon the great religious crisis of his life. A government official who was visiting him told about two army officers who had been so impressed by reading Athanasius' *Life of St. Anthony* that they had given up their army careers to become monks. Augustine felt deeply humbled when he heard this. Exposed to all the temptations of military life, these two men could deny themselves and take up the monastic life, while he with all his learning could not control his desires. As he was reflecting in the garden of his house on what he had heard, and feeling more deeply than ever his sinfulness and need of salvation, he suddenly heard a voice saying, "Take and read, take and read." He saw a Bible lying on a table, opened it, and read the first words that met his eye:

> For salvation is nearer to us now than when we first believed; the night is far gone, the day is at hand. Let us then cast off the works of darkness and put on the armor of light; let us conduct ourselves becomingly as in the day, not in reveling and drunkenness, not in debauchery and licentiousness, not in quarreling and jealousy. But put on the Lord Jesus Christ, and make no provision for the flesh, to gratify its desires. (Rom. 13:11-14)

Augustine's conversion dates from the moment of this reading, in the summer of 386. He immediately told his mother, who was filled with joy. He put away his concubine, and he requested Ambrose to instruct him for baptism, which he received in 386 in the cathedral of Milan, along with Adeodatus. In that same year Monica died, testifying to her faith and hope in God. The beloved Adeodatus, whose mind had much of the same brilliance as that of his father, died the following year at the age of eighteen.

After the moving experiences of his own birth to new life in Christ and the deaths of his mother and his son, Augustine returned to Africa. There he embarked upon the service of the Catholic Church and advanced rapidly in it. In 389 he was ordained a presbyter, in 395 the assistant bishop of Hippo, and a year later the full bishop. He lived a simple life in a monastery which he himself established. During the next thirty-five years he established himself as the theological center of the western church. Especially through his writings, he has exercised an influence that has endured to this day.

Augustine died in Hippo on August 28, 430, while the city was surrounded by the barbarian Vandals. A few months later, the city fell to them and was utterly destroyed. Only the cathedral and Augustine's library escaped the total destruction.

AUGUSTINE'S WRITINGS

The writings of Augustine are chiefly remembered for five

contributions he made to the life and thought of the church. These may be found in three separate books and in his writings against the Donatists and against Pelagius.

1. "The Confessions"

The first and best-known of the three books is his *Confessions*. In it Augustine examines his spiritual life and makes confession of his sins, but only in order to rightly confess God's praise. Each of these themes he sets forth in many places:

> Narrow is the mansion of my soul; enlarge Thou it, that Thou mayest enter in. It is ruinous; repair Thou it. It has that within which must offend Thine eyes; I confess and know it. But who shall cleanse it? or to whom shall I cry, save Thee? Lord, cleanse me from my secret faults and spare Thy servant from the power of the enemy. I believe and therefore do I speak. Lord, Thou knowest. Have I not confessed against myself my transgression unto Thee, and Thou, my God, hast forgiven the iniquity of my heart.

Further:

> O my God, let me with thanksgiving, remember and confess unto Thee Thy mercies on me. Let my bones be bedewed with my love, and let them say unto Thee, Who is like unto Thee, O Lord? Thou hast broken my bonds in sunder, I will offer unto Thee the sacrifice of Thanksgiving. And how Thou hast broken them I will declare; and all who worship Thee, when they hear this, shall say "Blessed be the Lord in heaven and earth, great and wonderful is His name."

Moving from childhood to manhood, from doubt to belief, he recalls small experiences and expresses the deepest thoughts. Augustine the man, the son, the friend, the philosopher and theologian, sees his own life and the lives of all men in the light of God. It is one of the great books of Christian devotion.

2. "The City of God"

The second book, *The City of God,* sets forth Augustine's view of history and its meaning. The writing of it was occasioned by the sack of Rome, the world's greatest city, in 410 by Alaric's Goths. This led many pagans, in Augustine's own words, to attribute this calamity to the Christian religion and began to blaspheme the true God. . . . It was this which kindled my zeal for the house of God, and prompted me to undertake the defense of the city of God against the charges and misrepresentations of its assailants.

Augustine acknowledges the greatness of Rome and the strength of Roman character that produced the city and its empire. But even the greatest of cities and nations must pass away. There is no human magnificence or achievement that lasts forever. Therefore we must look to the city of God, the New Jerusalem, which comes down from heaven. That city is now being built. It is the kingdom of God, the church of Christ, and it will endure forever. It exists as a city within the city of the world. Even in the church, not all are citizens of the kingdom of heaven. One day the city of evil, the kingdoms of man, will wholly disappear, and the city of God will shine in beauty forever.

3. "On the Trinity"

In his third book, *On the Trinity,* Augustine developed the final form of the western teaching regarding the Trinity. It will be remembered that Tertullian (in the West) and Origen (in the East) had viewed the Son as in some way subordinate to the Father. The Holy Spirit had not received much attention at all. Augustine developed the doctrine of the Trinity further in two ways. In the first place, he taught the full equality of the Father, the Son, and the Holy Spirit. There is no earlier or later, no superior or inferior, in the Trinity. The Son is fully God, and his distinctive character is to be eternally begotten by the Father. The Holy Spirit is fully God, and his distinctive character is to proceed from both the Father and the Son. Using a human example, Augustine illustrated the relationships within the Trinity by referring to the Father as the lover, the Son as the beloved one, and the Spirit as the love that unites them. In the second place, he related the Holy Spirit directly to the Son as well as to the Father. This is officially expressed in the Athanasian Creed (erroneously so called, since it was not written by Athanasius):

The Father is made of none, neither created nor begotten. The Son is of the Father alone; not made nor created, but begotten. The Holy Spirit is of the Father and of the

Son; neither made, nor created, nor begotten, but proceeding. . . . And in this Trinity none is afore, or after another; none is greater, or less than another. But the whole three persons are co-eternal, and co-equal. So that in all things, as aforesaid, the Unity in Trinity and the Trinity in Unity is to be worshiped.

The words "and of the Son" have been perpetuated in the famous Latin expression *filioque*. This teaching has been accepted in the western church but not in the eastern.

4. *"Against the Donatists"*

In the writings against the Donatists, Augustine set forth his doctrine of the church and the sacraments. The Donatists, the reader will recall, were orthodox in their teaching but did not recognize the Catholic Church. They had separated themselves from it because of the ordination of Caecilian as bishop of Carthage. His ordination, the Donatists claimed, was invalid because of the participation of Felix of Aptunga, who was accused of surrendering holy things to persecutors. They claimed that sacraments administered by an unworthy priest or by one who was ordained in an unworthy manner were thereby invalidated.

Augustine taught that the power of the sacraments does not lie in the character of the priest but in the character of the church. The Catholic Church is holy because it is apostolic; her bishops are successors of the apostles. Thus it is also unified and universal. There is no other church, and outside this church there is no salvation. For these reasons, its sacraments are holy and valid regardless of the character of the administering priest or minister. Augustine did not thereby approve of an immoral or unspiritual ministry. However, he did prepare the way for the rise of a ministry in which moral and spiritual worth was in danger of becoming less important than it ought to be.

5. *"Against the Pelagians"*

Pelagius, probably an Irish monk living in Rome, caused the greatest theological controversy in Augustine's time. He taught that God gave to every man the *possibility* of living a sinless life. This possibility is God's gift: man does not have it of himself. Further, man has the *will* to live such a life; this will is a part of man's being, for he has been created with it. Third, man has the *power* to actually lead a sinless life, a power he also has of himself. In short, man, without the strength and power from God, can by himself make the God-given possibility of leading a sinless life a reality, an actuality. Why then do men sin? They sin because of evil example. Sin is hence not an evil human condition from which men must be set free; it consists of separate evil actions. Man is by nature good, but his will to do good has been weakened by frequent yielding to evil example. The possibility of doing good with which man was created is assisted in two ways. God has given the law, and he has sent Christ to be our example. Baptism puts our shortcomings and failures behind us so that we are again free to fully do the good that God commands us to do.

For Augustine this doctrine contradicted both the teaching of Scripture and his own religious experience. Therefore, he replied to Pelagius (and his disciples Coelestius and Julian of Eclanum, both Italians) with the following principles. Sin does not consist in evil actions but in an evil nature inherited from Adam. Evil actions are caused by this evil nature. All men, without exception, are born with this evil nature. However, it is not a part of our created being; we received it after creation. Therefore, it can be removed and our original good nature restored to us. This restoration is the result of God's grace. Grace is God's work in the hearts of men that enables them to do good. Without it we cannot obey the law or believe the gospel of Christ. Belief in Christ unites us to him, adds love to faith, and makes possible a life of obedience to God. The grace of God is irresistible in those who are predestined to eternal life; it is not given to those who are predestined to eternal death.

The church accepted Augustine's teaching on sin and grace in its general outlines. It condemned Pelagianism at a synod held in Carthage in 416, and this decision was confirmed by Pope Innocent I. A second council held in 418 renewed the rejection, and this was endorsed by Pope Zosimus. A century later (in 529) a synod held in Orange, Gaul, further confirmed Augustine's teaching. It condemned, however, his teaching of predestination to eternal death and gave a prominence to good works that Augustine would not have approved. The Synod of Orange was a small gathering, but its importance was increased by the recognition that Pope Boniface II gave to its decisions. This became the Catholic position, until it was challenged by the Protestant Reformation of the sixteenth century.

6. Conclusion

The whole of Augustine's theology was deeply influenced by Greek Platonic philosophy in its later form, called Neo-Platonism. Before his conversion he had been a Manichaean, following the philosophy of Mani, a Persian thinker who died in 277. Its central teaching was the conflict between eternal good and eternal evil. In the new Platonism, Augustine learned that evil has no independent existence, that it is only the absence of good, that the world of real existence is the world of the spirit. It is in this light that he read the Bible, understood sin and grace, and viewed the Christian life. His long concern with Oriental and Greek thought probably contributed to his views on matters such as marriage, celibacy, asceticism, and monasticism. However, we must not be overly critical of this. Every generation of Christians is more or less deeply influenced by views of life and reality that are held by the leading thinkers of the day. This is unavoidable if the church is to speak to the world in which it lives.

QUESTIONS FOR REVIEW

1. Mention three unusual circumstances that attended the election of Ambrose as Bishop of Milan.

2. Describe Ambrose's attitude toward the Arians and toward the imperial government.

3. What characteristic feature of their age did Ambrose, Jerome, Chrysostom, and Augustine have in common? In what cities were they bishops? To what extent were they contemporaries?

4. What was the major contribution of Jerome to the life of the church? Why was it a lasting one?

5. What important lesson for all church leaders may be found in the life of Chrysostom?

6. What was the teaching of Pelagius, and why did Augustine take issue with it?

7. In his writings against the Donatists, what did Augustine teach about a) the sacraments, b) the ministry, and c) the unity of the church?

CHAPTER XIII

THE PROBLEM OF THE HUMAN AND THE DIVINE IN CHRIST

When the gospel came to the Greeks, they accepted it in faith and examined it with their intellect. Their faith produced the eastern church; their intellect produced eastern theology. With the aid of their theology, they studied the Christian faith, the central figure of which is Christ. It was to him that the Greeks gave all the attention of their deep minds. We have seen how they studied the relationship of the Son to the Father. During more than seventy years of discussion and debate, the church decided that Christ is: a) fully God, *homoousios* with the Father (i.e., of the same nature as the Father); and b) fully man, *homoousios* with our humanity. These were the decisions of Nicaea (325), which were confirmed by the Council of Constantinople (381). We traced this history in Chapter IX.

When this controversy ended, a new debate began. It concerned the relationship between the human nature and the divine nature in Christ. In one form or another, this controversy continued for more than four hundred years. During all these years ecclesiastical and imperial politics used theology for their own purposes. Out of these controversies arose much bitterness, persecution, and division in the church. Long before it was all over, the Muslims had overrun Palestine and Syria, as well as Egypt and North Africa. This was the beginning of the end for the church in those large and formerly fruitful Christian areas.

In concluding this book it is necessary to describe briefly the controversies about the natures of Christ. They do not come to an end until 787. In order to trace them to their conclusion, therefore, we shall at this point follow the story of the ancient church to the last quarter of the eighth century.

THE BEGINNING OF THE PROBLEM

When the fifth century began, the true deity and true humanity of Christ were universally believed in the Catholic Church.

However, it is possible to look at a common belief from various points of view. All the people of a country may believe that there should be both a national and a local form of government. But how are these to be related to each other? Where does the authority of the one end and that of the other begin? Are their duties clearly separated, or do they overlap? Similar questions arose in the church in connection with the human and the divine in Christ.

At the beginning of these discussions there were three general points of view about the relationship between them. They were not clearly expressed, however, and had to be worked out more carefully. This was done between the second ecumenical council held in Constantinople (381) and the sixth ecumenical council in Constantinople (680-681). Let us note the three views with which the discussions began.

1. The View of the West

The oldest of the three was the one held in the West; it was the position of Tertullian. He taught that the full divine nature and the full human nature were united unmixed in the one person, Jesus Christ. But who is this *person* in whom the two natures are united? Is it the Son who was with the Father from eternity? Is it the human being who was born of the virgin Mary? Or is it a combination of these two? These were questions to which Tertullian gave no final answers. They were also the questions around which much of the debate was to turn.

2. The View of Antioch

The second view was held at Antioch. There the theologians had from the beginning held a high regard for the work of God in human history. For this reason they saw the Bible not only as a book inspired by God but also as written by men, each with his own character, message, and historical circumstances. They emphasized the human life of Christ in the New Testament record of the Gospels. It was thus natural for them to give much weight to the human side of the life of our Lord. At the same time, they fully acknowledged his divine character. But how were they related in Christ so that he was not two beings but one?

3. The View of Alexandria

The third view was found in Alexandria. It arose out of

a certain conception of salvation. As we saw in Chapter IX, Athanasius looked on salvation as a work of God making the human divine. Its favorite text was II Peter 1:4, in which Peter speaks of the precious and very great promises God has given to us, "that through these you may escape from the corruption that is in the world because of passion, and become partakers of the divine nature." It was for this very reason that Athanasius fought so strongly against Arianism in order to defend the full deity of Christ. Only by union with a *divine* Savior could man obtain the immortality of God. For the same reason, the Christology of Alexandria gave more weight to the divine aspect of Christ than to the human. Would not such a strong emphasis on the divine thus be in danger of weakening or obscuring the teaching about the human side of Christ?

THE THEOLOGY OF THE PROBLEM

Such then were the various viewpoints in the church on the relationship of the human and the divine in Christ during the second half of the fourth century. The West left the problem open. Antioch tended to emphasize the human nature in Christ. Alexandria tended to emphasize the divine in Christ.

1. Apollinarius

It was in the year 360 that Apollinarius, bishop of Laodicea in Syria (about forty miles southwest of Antioch), made a careful attempt to solve the problem. He used the text of I Thessalonians 5:23 as a starting point. In it Paul speaks of man as consisting of "spirit and soul and body." Apollinarius taught that when the Son became man, the divine Reason or Logos took the place of the human spirit (i.e., the human mind or reason) in Jesus. Therefore, the man Jesus was fully divine in that he had the Logos, but he was incompletely human because he did not have a human mind or reason. This had been displaced by the divine mind.

The teaching of Apollinarius reminds us of the Christology of Arius. In his view, the reader will recall, the Logos took to himself only a human body, not a truly human being. Arius' Logos, moreover, was a creature. Arius' incarnate Son, therefore, was neither God nor man. Apollinarius' incarnate Son, on the other hand, was truly God; nevertheless he was not fully man. Consequently, the views of Apollinarius were condemned at the Council of Constantinople in 381.

2. The Weakness of the Antiochian View

After the rejection of the views of Apollinarius, Antioch and Alexandria advanced their teachings. The school of Antioch, of course, was very critical of Apollinarius. It believed in the true and full humanity of Christ. He was spirit, soul, and body united with the eternal Son of God, the Logos, the second person of the Trinity. Did two persons then dwell in him? No, said the Antiochians, the union between God and man is so complete that the two together make one being, one person. But how can two persons become one person? This problem became very great for the Antiochians, particularly when they discussed the suffering of Christ. In the Greek view, God could not suffer. Therefore, they said that God did not suffer in the sufferings of Christ; only the human part of Christ suffered. According to God's love, however, the divine love was present in the suffering, and thus God was present in the suffering. God was evidently present in Christ in some respects, but not in all respects. It is clear that the Antiochians did not succeed in keeping one united person. God and man dwelt together in Christ as two people dwell in a house. They may, like husband and wife, be very intimate; they may even be said to be "one." The fact is, however, that with respect to *person* they are not one but two. This was the weakness in the Antiochian teaching on the relationship of the two natures in Christ.

3. Cyril of Alexandria

Alexandria also faced the problem, and it was sympathetic to the teaching of Apollinarius because he strongly maintained and emphasized the deity of Christ. However, Alexandria did not agree with him that Christ lacked a human mind or reason. Alexandria, like Antioch, wanted the full divinity and the full humanity to be united in Christ. This required the inclusion in his being of a fully human mind or reason. The Alexandrians also objected to the weakness of the Antiochian view, in which the human and the divine in Christ did not appear to form a true unity. In trying to correct this error, they united the human and the divine in Christ so closely that the humanity was in danger of being swallowed up in the divinity.

This can be seen in the teaching of Cyril, patriarch of Alexandria from 412 to 444. He taught that the full humanity and the full divinity were united in Christ. That is to say, the Logos was united with humanity in body, soul, and spirit (reason or mind). In this respect he was at one with Antioch. But in a most important respect he differed from Antioch. In Cyril's view, the union of the two natures was so dominated by the divine that the humanity appeared to move into the background. He said, "One nature of the Word, and it made flesh." And again, "From two natures, one." The "one," however, was dominated by the Logos. Later, as we shall see, many of Cyril's followers went beyond him and taught that Christ had only one nature, namely a divine-human nature in which the human was swallowed up by the divine, as it were.

Thus, it is not surprising that in theological discussions, some began to speak of Mary, the mother of Jesus, as "Mother of God." Alexandria supported this. Antioch was naturally reluctant to use the expression. When it did use the expression "Mother of God," it always used careful exceptions, which did not please the Alexandrians. In the West, there was no serious problem. Moreover, the West was not divided as was the East. It followed men like Ambrose and Augustine. These in turn accepted the position of Tertullian, namely that in Christ a full and complete divine nature was united with a full and complete human nature, and that these two natures came to unified expression in the man Jesus Christ.

THE CHURCH'S ANSWER TO THE PROBLEM

Up to this point we have discussed only the theology of the two natures. In the early church, as we have noted repeatedly, theology seldom stood entirely on its own feet. It was often used as a means to advance ecclesiastical or imperial interests. It was in such a context that the church answered the problem of the two natures.

In 428, Nestorius, a noted preacher in the church at Antioch, became patriarch of Constantinople. He believed strongly in the Antiochian theology. Consequently, he was displeased when he heard many in the church in Constantinople refer to Mary as "Mother of God." This did not agree with the high regard in which the Antiochian teaching held the humanity of Christ. He preached against its use with all his eloquence.

In Constantinople and other parts of the East, especially in Alexandria, this seemed to be taking honor away from both Mary and Christ.

1. Politics in Ephesus

Cyril of Alexandria now saw an opportunity to humiliate both Constantinople and Antioch, advance his own theology, and extend the influence of Alexandria. He attacked Nestorius, saying that the latter taught only a human Savior. He wrote to the emperor, to the emperor's wife and sister, and to the Pope in Rome. Nestorius also appealed to the Pope, but he did so less diplomatically than Cyril. The view Nestorius held was a very mild form of Antiochian teaching; it came very close to the Roman view, perhaps closer than Cyril's view did. Nevertheless, Rome chose to support Alexandria. It probably did so because of political and ecclesiastical considerations rather than theological ones.

The eastern and western emperors together called a council to meet in Ephesus in 431. Cyril and his followers arrived before the supporters of Nestorius did, and Cyril called the council to meet without the participation of the Nestorians. In one day it condemned Nestorius and approved the Alexandrian position. When the delegates favorable to Nestorius arrived, he called his council and condemned Cyril. The emperor, and later the church, recognized Cyril's council even though it was illegal. Nestorius was retired to a monastery, but many of his followers remained faithful to him. They were persecuted in the empire but were received by the Persians. They also developed an extensive missionary activity that took Nestorianism as far as China in the seventh century.

In 433, Alexandria and Antioch came to a temporary agreement, but this was broken fifteen years later. In 448, a certain Eutyches, the aged abbot of a monastery in Constantinople, taught that at the Incarnation the two natures of Christ became united into one divine-human nature. There is some question whether he actually did teach this, but that was the official charge against him. This was a step further than Cyril had gone. The words of Eutyches were: "I confess that our Lord was of two natures before the union, but after the union one nature." A synod in Constantinople under the leadership of Flavian, the patriarch of Constantinople, condemned Eutyches. Both Eutyches and Flavian appealed to Pope Leo I in

Rome for an opinion. In response, Leo wrote his famous *Tome* (meaning large book), in which he set forth the western view of the natures of Christ.

At this point, Alexandria entered the controversy. Cyril had died in 444 and had been succeeded by Dioscorus. Like Cyril, he was trying to make Alexandria great by means of a theological victory. At his urgent request, the emperor called a council to meet in Ephesus in 449. Dioscorus completely controlled the situation. Eutyches was restored, and Flavian died a few months later. Leo's *Tome* was not even read. The meetings of the council were not orderly. Leo called it a "synod of robbers." The emperor, however, supported the decisions of the council. The victory of Alexandria was complete.

2. The Decisions of Chalcedon

In 450 the situation suddenly changed. The emperor, Theodosius II, died, and his sister Pulcheria and her husband Marcian now obtained the imperial power. Their sympathies were with Leo, who now requested a new council. The emperor called it in 451 to meet in Chalcedon, near Nicaea in Asia Minor. Six hundred bishops attended the assembly. All of them were from the East, except for the papal delegates sent by Leo. The council adopted the western position set forth by Leo in his *Tome*. Its basis was the Christology of Tertullian, but it went beyond him. Leo taught that in Christ were two complete natures, divine and human, and these were united in one person. This union was described with the use of four important words. The union of the two natures is *unmixed* and *unchanged; undivided* and *inseparable*. The first two, unmixed and unchanged, were directed against Alexandria, which tended to unite the two natures into one by mixing or changing them. The second two words, undivided and inseparable, were directed against Antioch, which tended to disunite the natures by dividing and separating them. The second important teaching of the *Tome* concerns the person in which the two natures are united. They are united in the person of the Son, "not parted or divided into two persons, but one and the same Son and only-begotten, God the Word, the Lord Jesus Christ."

These positions of Leo's *Tome* became the decisions of Chalcedon. The decisions of Chalcedon were on the one hand wise, but on the other hand incomplete. The wisdom of Chalcedon is that it did not attempt to say *how* the natures are united in Christ. Rather, it warned against how they are *not* united. The crucial words of Chalcedon are all negative words. To Alexandria the council said that the two natures are *not* mixed and *not* changed; to Antioch it said that the two natures are *not* divided and *not* separated. Beyond this it did not go.

That the decision of the council was incomplete will be clear when we compare it with the teachings of Apollinarius. For him, the divine Logos took the place of the human logos or mind. This left the humanity of Christ incomplete, and for that reason the church rejected the teaching of Apollinarius. Chalcedon confessed the full divinity of Christ and the full humanity: it considered Christ to have a fully human mind as well as a fully human soul and body. The *person* of Christ, however, is divine, not human. Therefore, the problem of Apollinarius remained, but at a different level — the level of the person instead of the level of mind. It is perhaps not too strong to say that the problem can never disappear. When the Creator becomes one with the creature, the eternal with the temporal, the divine with the human, we can never fully answer the question, How can this be? All the wisdom of the theologians cannot go beyond the simple words of John: "And the Word became flesh and dwelt among us, full of grace and truth."

The Council of Chalcedon also had great ecclesiastical significance. Dioscorus was deposed, which was a great humiliation for Alexandria. Rome stood first in theological wisdom in the church, but Constantinople was declared to be equal in dignity with Rome, to which Leo strongly objected. Jerusalem was made a patriarchate, leaving four patriarchates in the East, while Rome alone ruled all the West.

THE PROBLEM REMAINS

The church's official decisions of a doctrinal character have value if the church believes them. If not, many will not accept the decisions. The decree of Nicaea was followed by nearly sixty years of controversy. A similar result followed the decision of Chalcedon.

1. The Monophysite Controversy
Many followers of Cyril felt that the council had not fully

rejected the teachings of the Antiochian school. They believed that at the Incarnation the two natures of Christ became one combined divine-human nature. They were willing to say that the one combined nature of Christ came *out of* two natures. They were not willing to say, as Chalcedon did, that Christ always has two natures. Therefore, they were called Monophysites (from *mono* meaning one, plus *phusis* meaning nature). The Monophysites were strong in Syria, Palestine, and Egypt. Efforts at reconciliation were not successful.

In 527 a great emperor ascended the throne: Justinian, who reigned until 565. He had the grand plan of gaining the western part of the empire back from the Germans. In order to do this, he needed united support. Since religion was the strongest force in the empire, he felt that he had to become master of the church. To do so, he had to enforce the decrees of Chalcedon. The West, of course, agreed with Chalcedon; the orthodox part of the East also accepted it. However, the Monophysites did not, and they were numerous and influential. In order to gain their support, Justinian rejected the writings of three prominent Antiochian theologians of the previous century. This led to a controversy called the "Three Chapters," which referred to the teachings of the three theologians. In 553, Justinian called the fifth general council to meet in Constantinople. It condemned the "Three Chapters" and thereby made it almost necessary to read the decisions of Chalcedon as in accordance with the views of Cyril. Those who would not agree were persecuted.

This controversy had far-reaching consequences. In Egypt, the entire Christian population was Monophysite; in effect they formed a separate church. In Syria, the Monophysites also formed a separate communion, known as the Jacobite Church (after their early leader, Jacob Baradaeus). Armenia and Ethiopia also became Monophysite.

2. The Two Wills Controversy

The Monophysite controversy did not signal the end of the disputes concerning the natures of Christ. There were two more to come. The first was the question whether there was one or two wills in Christ. This caused so much unrest that in 638 the emperor Heraclius forbade any discussion of it, saying at the same time that Christ had one will. This was clearly a Monophysite position. In 648 the emperor Constans repeated the prohibition. In 649, Rome, supporting Chalcedon against the Monophysites, declared that Christ had two wills. All the important Monophysite areas—Egypt, Syria, and Palestine—were now under Muslim control. The Muslims threatened the empire in North Africa and Asia Minor. Agreement with Rome was therefore desirable. In 680-681 the emperor called the sixth general council to be held in Constantinople. It approved the Roman view that Christ had "two natural wills. . . . His human will follows . . . subject to his divine and omnipotent will." This decision finally brought to an end the doctrinal, or theological, aspect of the long debate about the two natures of Christ.

3. The Picture Controversy

However, there was an unexpected postscript to the controversy. In 717 a powerful emperor, Leo the Isaurian, began to reign. He was concerned about the spiritual condition of the church. He was also eager to be master of the church as Justinian had been. As a means to strengthen spiritual living in the church, and to give him control over it, he forbade the worship of images and pictures of divine persons or things. He enforced this decree with the use of the army. He was generally successful, but the West did not agree and many in the East refused to obey him.

Those who were against images said that images took the place of heathen idols and that Scripture forbade their use. Supporters of images (and also pictures) said that material things can be pictures of the immaterial God and his work of salvation. Moreover, they stated that "the emperor's sphere is the right conduct of political affairs; the management of ecclesiastical affairs is the province of pastors and teachers." At bottom, the problem was that of monophysitism. If the human is altogether overshadowed by the divine in Christ, then we should not make material images of spiritual things. Worship should be wholly spiritual. The political implication of this was that the church should be concerned only with religious, that is, spiritual matters. Affairs of this life should be governed by the state. That is why Leo introduced pictures and images of himself everywhere. (He was also concerned about the fact that the church had a great deal of property and that its clergy was exempt from the taxes that other citizens had to pay.) On the other hand, if the human in Christ is as real as the divine, then the things that are created and material can help us worship the Creator and appreciate the spiritual. It was this view that prevailed in the end.

In 787 the Roman emperor Constantine VI called the seventh general council to meet in Nicaea to settle the issue. It decreed that pictures, the cross, and the Gospels "should be given due salutation and reverence. . . . For the honour which is paid to the image passes on to that which the image represents, and he who shows reverence to the image shows reverence to the subject represented in it." Thus, in 787 the Christological disputes came to an end. For four hundred sixty years they had been the center of ecclesiastical and imperial politics. All seven councils had been called by emperors, and toward the end the emperors themselves had become theologians and were publishing theological and ecclesiastical decrees. All the councils were caused by controversies in the East, and they were all held in the East. Yet in their most crucial decisions the Roman view was decisive.

The Christological controversies began and ended in Nicaea. They began on the high and lofty level of the eternal relationship between the Father and the Son. They ended with the decision that Christians may reverence pictures of the Father, the Son, and other spiritual realities. Between the first council and the last lay the increasingly peculiar debates about the two natures in Christ, the one person of Christ, the one will and the two wills of Christ. While the last controversies were in progress, large sections of the empire were being lost to the Muslims. Monophysite and Nestorian churches had come into being. The eastern and western churches had grown apart and were finally to separate in 1054.

We leave our review of the development and life of the ancient church with gratitude to God for all that he gave to Christians through those first centuries of the church's life. We leave it also with humility and a certain fear when we contemplate what the church has done with those gifts. We leave it no less with hope and confidence in him who is the beginning and the end, the first-born from the dead, and the ruler of the kings of the earth, who will — in spite of us — complete the building of his body, which is the church of the living God.

THE SEVEN ECUMENICAL COUNCILS

The following chart lists the seven ecumenical councils, their dates, and the decisions that were made:*

I	Nicaea	325	Declared the Son *homoousios* with the Father.
II	Constantinople	381	Confirmed Nicaea and concluded the Arian controversy.
III	Ephesus	431	Rejected Nestorius and endorsed the Alexandrian view of the relationship between the two natures of Christ.
IV	Chalcedon	451	Completed discussion on the relationship between the two natures of Christ with the words *unmixed, unchanged; unseparated, undivided.*
V	Constantinople	553	Rejected three prominent Antiochian theologians (the "Three Chapters"), and thereby endorsed the Cyrillian understanding of Chalcedon.
VI	Constantinople	680-681	Accepted two wills in Christ.
VII	Nicaea	787	Declared the reverencing of pictures and images of divine realities legitimate.

*The council held in 449, which Pope Leo called the "robbers' synod," is not regarded as a legitimate ecumenical council.

QUESTIONS FOR REVIEW

1. How would you formulate the difference between the problem about Christ which confronted the Council of Nicaea and that which confronted the Council of Chalcedon?

2. What were the Christological viewpoints of the West, of Antioch, and of Alexandria at the end of the fourth century?

3. How did Apollinarius try to solve the problem? Why did he not succeed?

4. What was the weakness of the view of Antioch?

5. Alexandria recognized the weakness of the Antioch position, but how did this create its own weakness?

6. How did the Council of Chalcedon resolve the difficulty? Against what views are its four central words directed?

7. How did church and imperial politics influence the history of the problem from 430 to 451? What role did Rome have in the decision of the Council of Chalcedon?

8. Indicate the forms in which the Christological problem continued in the life of the church.

9. How did Muslims contribute to the ending of the controversy?

BIBLIOGRAPHY

I. *General Reading*
Bruce, F. F. *The Spreading Flame*. London: Paternoster, 1958.
Eusebius. *The History of the Church from Christ to Constantine*, tr. G. A. Williamson. New York: New York Univ. Press, 1966.
Foakes-Jackson, F. J. *History of the Christian Church to AD 461*. London: Allen and Unwin, repr. 1965.
Foster, John. *After the Apostles, Missionary Preaching of the First Three Centuries*. London: SCM, 1951.
Idem. The First Advance, AD 29-500, TEF Study Guide 5. London: S.P.C.K., 1972.
Frend, W. H. C. *The Early Church*. Philadelphia and New York: Lippincott, 1966.
Heick, O. W. *A History of Christian Thought*, Vol. I. Philadelphia: Fortress, 1965.
Latourette, K. S. *A History of the Expansion of Christianity*, Vol. I, *The First Five Centuries*. Grand Rapids: Zondervan, repr. 1973.
Walker, Williston. *A History of the Christian Church*, Revised Edition. New York: Scribner's, 1959.
Wand, J. W. C. *A History of the Early Church*, 4th Edition. London: Methuen, 1963.

II. *Documents*
Bettenson, H. S. *Documents of the Christian Church*. London: Oxford Univ. Press, 1956.
Stevenson, J. *A New Eusebius, Documents Illustrative of the History of the Church to 337*. London: S. P. C. K., 1960.

III. *For More Advanced Study*
Bury, J. B. *The Invasion of Europe by the Barbarians*. New York: Norton, 1967.
Cross, F. L., ed. *The Oxford Dictionary of the Christian Church*. London: Oxford Univ. Press, 1958.
Grant, R. M. *Gnosticism and Early Christianity*, 2nd Edition. New York: Columbia Univ. Press, 1966.
Idem. Gnosticism, An Anthology, ed. R. M. Grant. London: Collins, 1961.
Greenslade, S. L. *Schism in the Early Church*. London: SCM, 1953.
Harnack, Adolf. *The Mission and Expansion of Christianity in the First Three Centuries*, Vol. I, tr. and ed. James Moffatt. New York: Harper Torchbook, 1961.
Lietzmann, H. *A History of the Early Church*, 5 vols., tr. Bertram

Lee Wolf. London: Lutterworth, 1938ff.

Schaff, Philip. *History of the Christian Church* (of which Vols. I, Il, III deal with the early Church). Grand Rapids: Eerdmans, 1955.

Seeberg, R. *Textbook of the History of Doctrines,* tr. Charles E. Hay. Grand Rapids: Baker, 1966.

INDEX

Achamoth, 57-59

Adoptionism, 111-112

Aeons, gnostic beings, 57-59

Against the Donatists, by Augustine of Hippo, 161

Against the Pelagians, by Augustine of Hippo, 161-163

Alexander, bishop of Alexandria, 115-116

Alexander the Great, 4

Alexandria
center for the Christian church, 24-25
center of the Jewish Dispersion, 7
Christological emphasis in, 166-168, 170-172
development of church in, 80, 90-94

Ambrose, bishop of Milan, 148-150, 158

Anaximander, 7-8

Anicetus, bishop of Rome, 83

Anthony, first Christian monk, 129

Antioch
Christological emphasis in, 170-172
description of, 155
Paul's arrival in, 23

Antiochus IV, king of Syria, 4

Antonian monasticism, 129-130

Apollinarius, bishop of Laodicea, 167-168

Apollos, 24

Apologists, Christian, 48-52
Trinitarian position of, 110-113

Apostles' Creed, 73-77

Apostolic Fathers, 31-35, 109

Apostolicity, 72

Arian missions, 125-127

Arianism
Athanasian opposition to, 167
Council of Constantinople and, 120
Council of Nicea and, 115-118
description of, 113-114
Jesus according to, 114-118
threat to the gospel, 10

Aristotle, 9

Arius
Athanasius' relationship to teachings of, 117

Council of Nicea and, 115, 117
teachings of, 113-114

Armenia, church in, 25

Asceticism, 128-129

Athanasian Creed, 160

Athanasius
Constantine II and Constans support, 117
enemy of Arianism, 167
Julian the Apostate and, 118
New Testament collection of, 72-73
relation to Athanasian Creed, 160
theology of, 116-117, 119

Athens, cultural center of the ancient world, 9

Atheoi, 46

Augustine, bishop of Hippo
Ambrose as the teacher of, 149
ecclesiastical figure, 85, 148
establishment of New Testament Canon, 72
life of, 156-158
Trinitarian views of, 119
writings of, 158-161

Baptism
in mystery religions, 13
sacramental, 144-145
spoken of in *The Shepherd,* by Hermas, 32, 34, 39

Barnabas of Alexandria, 31-32, 34

Basil of Caesarea, 119

Benedictine monasticism, 131-132

Benedict of Nursia, 130-132

Bishop, office of, 28-32, 68-71, 139

Bishop of Rome, 70

Burgundians, 127

Caecilian, 137-138

Caesar Augustus (Octavianus), 2

Carthage, church in, 80, 83-90

Cerdo, the gnostic, 60

Chalcedon, Fourth Ecumenical Council, 171-174, 176

Christ
forming an acceptable Christology,

as used by Clement of Alexandria, 91

Gnosticism
as threat to gospel, 10
description of, 55-60
Irenaeus' opposition to, 69
Jesus of, 58
NT as answer to, 71

Goths, 123
Greek philosophers, early, 7-11
Gregory of Nazianzus, 119
Gregory of Nyssa, 119

Hadrian, emperor, 100
Hebrew Christians, 18-21
Hellenist Christians, 18-21
Heraclitus, 7-9
Hermas of Rome, 31-32, 34, 39
Hexapla, by Origen, 92
Holy days, 146-147
Holy places, 146-147
Homoiousios, 118-119
Homoousios, 116-117, 119, 165
Hosius, bishop of Cordova, 115, 117
Huns, 123

Ignatius, bishop of Antioch
authority of the bishop according to, 29, 31-32, 68-70
authority of Rome as evidenced in letter by, 82
desire for martyrdom of, 33, 82
der, 91

Instructor, The, by Clement of Alexandria, 91

Irenaeus, bishop of Lyons
authority of bishops according to, 69-70
interpretation of the Apostles' Creed by, 76
opposition to gnosticism by, 60
opposition to Marcion by, 61
Quartodeciman controversy and, 83
Trinitarian views of, 110-111

Irish monasticism, 132
Israel, 3, 5, 15, 17

Jerome, translator of the Latin Bible, 151-154

Jesus
Arian teaching concerning, 114-118
Gnostic teaching concerning, 58
ministry of, 15-16
Jewish background, 3-7
Julian the Apostate, 118, 140
Justin Martyr, 48-51, 110

Leo I, Pope, 170-171
Leo the Isaurian, 174-176
Libanius, 154
Libellus, 87
Licinius, 105

Logos
Apollinarius' concept of, 167-168, 172
Arian concept of, 113-114
Clement of Alexandria's concept of, 91
Heraclitus' concept of, 8
Justin Martyr's concept of, 110
Paul of Samosata's concept of, 113
Philo's concept of, 11
Stoic concept of, 11

Maccabees, 45
Mani, 163
Manicheans, 163
Marcion, 60-63, 71
concept of Christ, 62
Marcionism, 55, 60-63
Marcus Aurelius, Roman emperor, 11, 100
Marjorinus, 138
Mark, 24
Marriage, among Christians, 37-38
Martyrdom, desire for, 33
Mary, mother of Jesus, 145, 169
Maxentius, 105
Maximian, 98, 103-106
Maximin Daia, 104-105
Metropolitan bishop, office of, 30
Miscellanies, by Clement of Alexandria, 91
Mithraism, 13
Modalistic monarchianism, 112
Monarchical bishop, office of, 29-30, 68-69, 135

Monasticism
European, 130-132
rise of, 127-132

Monica, mother of Augustine of Hippo, 157-158
Monophysite controversy, 172-174

Montanism
explanation of, 63-65
influence of, 65
North African, 85
threat to the church, 55

Montanus, 63-64
Muratorian fragment, 72
Mystery religion, 12-13, 55

Nature religion, 12, 55
Nero, Roman emperor, 27, 42, 100